ROACH

ROACH

The Gentle Giants

John Bailey

The Crowood Press

First published in 1987 by
The Crowood Press
Ramsbury, Marlborough,
Wiltshire SN8 2HE

British Library Cataloguing in Publication Data

Bailey, John
Roach: The gentle giants
1. Roach fishing
I. Title
799.1'752   SH691.R6
ISBN 1 85223 035 5

Black and White Picture Credits
Laurence Ashley, page 132; John Cadd, page 125; Martin
James, page 18; Dave Phillips, page 43; Roy Shaw, pages 120,
121 and 122; Gerry Swanton, page 98; John Wilson, pages 45,
86 and 89; Owen Wentworth, pages 97, 99, 100, 103 and
104; others by the author.

Typeset by Inforum Ltd
Printed in Great Britain

Contents

Preface

Giants? Oh yes! There are those fishermen who never have the fortune to see a big roach – a roach of over a pound, of two pounds, or even of the fabled three. They miss a sight of real wonder and to their dying days they will hardly believe roach can grow so large. By good luck, with a dash of skill, very many of us do catch such roach and we feel all our time is well spent on what are the greatest of fish.

That roach are gentle, no one would deny. They are the most serene of all our coarse fish. They graze the underwater world with all the calm of horses at pasture. Look into the eye of an eighteen-year-old roach and you have an insight into a wisdom that has accepted diseases, droughts and pike attacks with stoic resignation. When such a fish dies, the river bed receives it and day by day covers it in the finest silt whilst the alders and the willows wish it farewell.

Introduction

There is some justification in my writing a book on roach fishing. I have certainly studied the species in some depth, over some time, in many places. I have fished for roach for thirty-one years. Using the diaries and records that I have not lost, I have probably taken a roach rod out on between three and three and a half thousand sessions. That makes a total of about twelve thousand hours of fishing, or a continuous five hundred days, or an unbroken eighteen months – every second after roach.

I cannot count the number of small pools, ponds and meres from which I have caught roach, but the number of canals is five, the number of pits nearly fifty and larger lakes around thirty. I can also count my rivers up to

One of the most beautiful roach from thirty-one years' fishing – an immaculate fish of 2lb 9oz.

thirty: the Dane, Weaver, Trent, Ure, Aire, Nidd, Tweed, Tay, Endrick, Ouse, Nar, Wissey, Wensum, Glaven, Bure, Yare, Waveney, Tay, Thames, Kennet, Stour, Avon, Wye, Lugg, Blackwater, Shannon, Ribble, Lune and the Loire and Cher in France. As for reservoirs, I have taken roach from Ardleigh, Abberton and Alton Water.

These efforts have produced four 3lb roach from rivers and one from stillwaters. There have been a further four hundred roach over 2lb and, even more approximately, another nine hundred over 1lb. All in all, this makes very close to one ton of good roach.

Why roach have had this effect on me is not immediately easy to tell. Even a three-pounder is not large as fish go. Roach do not fight especially impressively, and an aching rod arm belongs more to the tench, carp or barbel man. But, in colour and shape, I believe a big roach is one of the most beautiful coarse fish. They are also one of the most difficult to catch. They are not greedy and they are constantly alert. A clumsy presentation or a heavy approach is more fatal with roach than with almost any other species. In short, they are a magnificent and worthwhile quarry.

Finally, having explained my credentials and the attraction of roach, I should explain why a book on them is necessary. In the 1960s and 1970s, roach were probably one of the leading specialist species. A great number of men spent a great deal of time pursuing them – and still do. This book attempts to record this knowledge for what remains of the 1980s and for those anglers coming on in the 1990s. I do not want the experience of men like Wilson, Miles, Wentworth, Swanton or Mousley to be lost.

As I write in 1986, carp, pike and barbel are the dominating quarry of those seeking better fish. The wheel is turning, however. I hope this book speeds the revolution and brings the roach back to where it belongs – in the forefront of the specialist angling world.

The North West

BEGINNINGS

I began to fish for the roach of the North West in 1955. There followed an intensive decade until 1966, when I moved on and have never once returned. After twenty years away, I have little constructive to say about waters and techniques current in that region today. What does remain is a glitter of memories that show why I became a roach man. These were the formative years and everything that I learned and experienced burns as brightly, untarnished by the passing years. My very first roach was a triumph, still locked away in my heart, still relived with that euphoria all true anglers recognise.

Roach – a profile of this, the 'real fish'.

It had been a struggle, that first roach from the Peak Forest Canal. The step from stickleback and gudgeon to 'real' fish had taken me a whole year. Tiny, aware, ever alert, canal roach would not tolerate my initial clumsiness, but first my casting improved, then my bait presentation, and all the time the distance between us narrowed. The forces pulled us towards a certain summer night . . .

Twilight and on into darkness are the very best hours for roach. Of this I have no doubt now, and I suspected it then, thirty years ago. Dawn is good, and they can be caught through drizzly, grey days, but no time compares with the hours of gathering darkness. My very first roach taught me that.

June. A Friday evening, warm, still, with a dusk that never ended and a nightfall that was barely noticeable. In the calm, the reflection of the mill was perfect across the canal and my red crow-quill lay atop its 100-foot chimney. Only sticklebacks bothered me until sunset and then they went quiet. The night tingled with the smell of monsters. The quill's moment had come. It cocked and slid away somewhere down into that dark factory. To me, that roach was huge. At 5oz, it confirmed me as a roach man for life.

Sometime around 1959, I joined my first angling club. It owned a single water – a storage reservoir hacked into the steep hillside and flanked by terraces of weavers' cottages. A pigeon fancier had his cots at the head of the water where the sheep field came down. Over his pipes he told me about the slack times in the mills, about wars, about bets and how to look for cheats.

On three sides, gardens and allotments adjoined the banks, always busy with women and their washing, old men and their vegetables. I remember one dark haired woman in particular. A certain window cleaner was her constant companion and when he saw me he came through the gate.

He taught me the fixed spool reel, how to use the clutch and give line to a running fish. Due to him, I bought a landing net and a 'man's' 13-foot rod, but above all, he quickened my taste for mystery. He told me of massive, uncaught, unsuspected roach in the deep water. Each evening I left, thrilled.

The second or third summer, the club held its 'Open'. Along with forty rough hands, I dipped into the bag for my peg number. I drew the high bank by the sycamore trees – a place forbidden to me before because of the 12-foot drop to the water. It was a special day, warm with high cloud. The women leaned over every gate. The fancier put £1 on me to win, and the window cleaner sat down behind me, telling me to go deeper, to change baits, to put in a little feed or to go finer as the sun climbed.

Twelve small perch, and I was in the lead. As each shiny fish was pulled up the wall the fancier clapped and the women cheered, but the miracle was still to come.

*Every young angler in the 1950s had a copy of Crabtree by his
bedside.*

'*On the strike, a roach emerged . . .*'

A little before the whistle, the float trembled. On the strike a roach emerged, so huge a quietness fell on the dam. Never could I lift such a fish on fine gear and the net was 6-foot too short. The window cleaner left for his van. I began to panic and the dark haired woman calmed me down. I started to play the fish out and it was on its side when the window cleaner returned – with his ladder. He slid it into the water, propped it against the wall and was there with net at water level. He scooped the roach up, held it aloft and the whole valley cried in triumph. It weighed 1lb 14oz 12 dr. I was a big roach man now. I knew my future.

About that time, I had a hero, the greatest roach man of all: Albert. I had met him now and again, but never dared speak until one February night. The day had begun early for me because I wanted roach, wanted so much to be as successful as Albert, that I got up and cranked the bike down the cobbled lane to the canal long before sunrise.

The Peak Forest Canal on a miserable February dawn.

First light was breaking as I tackled up. Nothing bright or cheerful, just a glimmering to let me see the water unfrozen under the far trees and the damp snow on the branches and the mill roof. I was laying on double maggot, a size 16 under a quill the size of a matchstick – all as tight and light as I could make it, with just a pinch of maggots around the swim from time to time. I was getting sticklebacks all day and one gudgeon, which seemed a miserable, mottled, smelly old thing after making my heart beat for a second.

By midday I was frightened, thinking Albert would come and that I would not have a roach in the net to show him. I half decided to pack up rather than meet him, the great one, without a roach to my name. Miserable, though, I continued.

About three, I got my first roach – about two ounces – and into the net it went. Not much, but I could pretend I had just fished a short session. They just kept coming though, those roach, as the light failed. Each cast the tiny quill would cock, move three inches against the ripple, be away down to the depths and I'd be in again!

Now I prayed for Albert to come, to see this, to see I could fish, could catch roach. At last his bike sounded in the gloom and along the tow-path he rattled.

I tried to be casual over my catch, but just could not, and when he leaned on the wall behind me to watch, my heart nearly stopped. He netted a roach for me, *for me*. Albert – Albert Oldfield. He applauded when I struck on a hunch and hit a six-ouncer. Albert Oldfield applauded – the man who wrote for the press, the man who had caught a three-pounder!

When it came to pack up, he helped me to count the fish and patted me on the back. He patted me – Albert Oldfield. Then, as bailiff not hero, he sold me a ticket, issued by the County Palatine for one shilling. He got on to his bike, pushed off and called 'Look in the *Times* on Friday'.

The cutting in the *Angling Times* river reports that Friday read: 'Local schoolboy John Bailey caught twenty roach up to 1lb on double maggot at Oakwood Mill'. I was not just a big roach man now. I was a *famous* big roach man, hooked well and truly for life!

BETTER ROACH FISHING IN THE NORTH WEST

Martin James

The North West of England has probably more anglers than any other area of the country, but it is also one of the poorest areas for big fish. We don't have the big gravel pit chains or rich reservoirs of the Midlands and the South, most of the waters have a very low pH, the acidity is usually high and many waters are preserved for the salmon and trout fishermen. These are not the best conditions for us big roach anglers – and by big roach, I mean over 1lb 8oz.

Big roach fishing in the North West is improving as we go into the late 1980s and early 1990s, with rivers becoming much cleaner and new stillwaters being opened up for coarse fishing. However, the big question is, will this improvement continue, with the twin evils of water abstraction and pollution an ever-present threat? There are lots of rivers in the North West, but only four of them interest us big roach anglers: the Dane in Cheshire and the Wyre, Lune and Ribble in Lancashire, and it is the last two that can produce quality roach, equal to most places in the country. However, whereas anglers in the South fish for roach with bread baits, their northern counterparts fish a single maggot on a 20 hook – not the usual method for big roach in the 1980s and 1990s, so not many of the Ribble roach are caught.

The roach fishing is improving all the time. As the 6 to 8oz fish have disappeared, so 1lb 8oz to 2lb roach have increased in numbers. Every year the big Ribble roach are reported in the press, and although the odd ones turn out to be chub, there are plenty of fully authenticated catches of big roach. Some of the big Ribble roach are taken on fly, by the game angler, especially those who fish the Dinkley stretch above Ribchester which is controlled by a game fishing club. I would give my right arm to fish this stretch during the autumn and winter with bread baits, lobworms and sweetcorn.

Roach fishing on the Ribble stretches from Dinkley downstream to Preston, Ribchester, Osbaldeston Hall, Sunderland Hall, Stubbins Wood, Alston Old Hall, Elston, Red Scar Wood, and The Tickled Trout, and it is

17

*Martin James holds a
Ribble fish of 2lb 4½oz*

from these areas that most of the big catches of quality roach are taken. Many of these fish are caught by chub anglers fishing with bread baits. Over the past three seasons I have been fishing for the big Ribble roach using crust flake, lobworm tails, sweetcorn and very small redcap boilie baits, and found that a lot of the better roach are quite young fish, which augurs well for the future. I've found pre-baiting with corn helps a lot, though you can get problems with chub at times. Fishing during the evenings in winter, sport has been very good, with three or four roach around the pound and a half mark being taken.

   If you can catch the river carrying about six inches of extra fresh water, with the wind from the South West, take a loaf of bread and be there for dusk – you can have a good evening's sport with the roach and the chances of fish over 2 pounds exist. In the not too distant future, the river will give up one of its jewels, a 3lb roach, providing we don't get a bout of pollution.

   The next water on my list is the River Lune, mostly a game fishing water

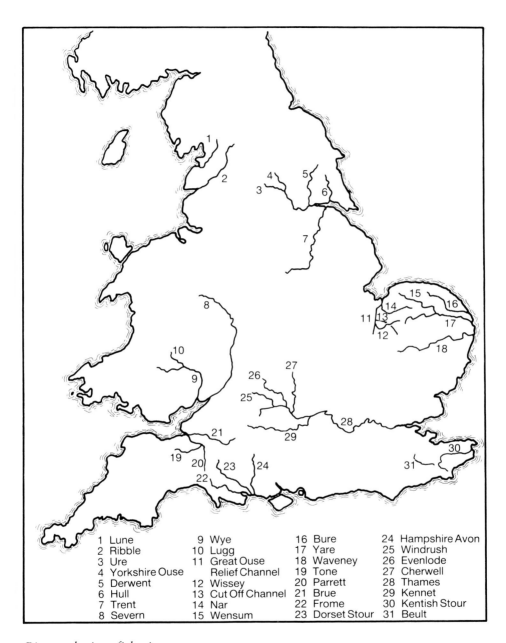

1 Lune
2 Ribble
3 Ure
4 Yorkshire Ouse
5 Derwent
6 Hull
7 Trent
8 Severn

9 Wye
10 Lugg
11 Great Ouse
    Relief Channel
12 Wissey
13 Cut Off Channel
14 Nar
15 Wensum

16 Bure
17 Yare
18 Waveney
19 Tone
20 Parrett
21 Brue
22 Frome
23 Dorset Stour

24 Hampshire Avon
25 Windrush
26 Evenlode
27 Cherwell
28 Thames
29 Kennet
30 Kentish Stour
31 Beult

Big roach river fisheries.

but it has a reputation for producing big roach. What is more incredible is that only a short stretch above and below the M6 motorway bridge actually holds the quality roach. The North West roach record is 3lb 4oz and it was captured from the River Lune just above the M6 motorway bridge. Several 2lb fish are being caught each season and the prospects for the future look good. The only problem is if a chemical tanker should have a spillage on the M6 in the vicinity of the motorway bridge.

Lansil Angling Club control the fishing rights up and downstream of the M6 on the south bank. The Lansil stretch of water is completely different from the rest of the River Lune. It is very slow and deep and lots of silt has collected, so there is good weed growth, very different from the River Lune so often featured with game anglers along its banks.

The top two methods for roach fishing are long-range waggler fishing with caster and bread baits or swingtipping and quivertipping. Sweetcorn dyed red has helped me get some better quality fish and the best time is at dusk.

This beat of water is wide and featureless and the newcomer to the Lune would be well advised to seek local advice if it is big roach he wants. This stretch of the Lune should be your choice and, being so close to the motorway, it is so easy to reach from any direction. As with all big fish waters it is hard fishing, but the rewards can be great; I would not be surprised to see a 3lb 8oz roach taken over the next three or four years. If it is a summer caught fish, bread crust or flake will be the bait, but during the late autumn or winter when the water is coloured and the small eels have disappeared, the two baits *par excellence* are redworms or a 2-inch lobworm tail or head – yes, the head of a lobworm is also a good bait!

Two other North West rivers that produce the odd good roach are Lancashire's River Wyre and Cheshire's River Dane. However, as the chub shoals increase on these two rivers, so I'm afraid the roach will suffer. The reason the roach survive and are growing big on the Ribble is that it is a big water that can accommodate both the chub and roach. We will continue to catch the odd good fish from the Wyre and Dane, but prospects are better on the Lune or Ribble.

When you look at the map, you see several canals throughout the North West, but with the increase in boat traffic, the roach fishing has deteriorated and the serious roach angler steers clear of the canals. In the late 1970s the roach fishing in the Rochdale Canal between Todmorden and Hebden Bridge was equal to any venue in the country, with numerous roach over 2lb being caught. Andrew Gallagher of Burnley and myself pre-baited two swims every evening during the last two weeks of August with 2lb sweetcorn, then fished it during September with great success, catching large numbers of roach over 1lb 8oz, with many over 2lb. My best was 2lb 7oz, but then, in the name of progress, the lengths were drained and excavated to allow the passage of boats; now the canal is like any other in the North West, useless.

STILLWATER ROACH

The North West is certainly not lacking in stillwater fisheries, from small mill lodges to large reservoirs and meres. Cheshire has several meres which are what I would call average roach fishing waters. They do not produce big roach in any quantity, but the odd 2lb fish is taken each year. I don't see the picture improving greatly, though I would like to be proved wrong, as lots of the Cheshire waters are very picturesque. I love fishing these waters but big roach are not the fish to seek, unless you know one that is consistently producing better roach. Please let me know if you do!

One water that has hit the headlines over the past couple of years is a large limestone pit at Carnforth, alongside the M6 north of Lancaster. It has

Sharon Bailey cradles a 2lb 6oz stillwater roach.

produced a lot of big roach up to 2lb 9oz, but 3lb roach are on the cards. You don't catch many small roach. Most fish are 1lb or more and the reason for the lack of small roach and the excellent head of big roach is the large head of cormorants that visit the water. This is gin clear and it is these birds feeding on the small roach that produce the big roach, as only a few of the small ones survive. The water is deep, around twenty feet along the bank next to the M6 and it is this bank that produces most fish. Sometimes an angler will take 30lb or more of roach at a sitting.

Dockacre has a great future as a big roach water, and providing bream are not introduced the roach will prosper. Who knows, it could produce a new roach record? The big roach that have been caught are all young fish in pristine condition. Without doubt it is the North West's top big roach water, but commercialisation of this fishery could be the end of the roach fishing – the owners already allow fishing to go on during the close season, on the pretext of trout fishing. This should be stopped once and for all. There are plenty of trout-fishing-only waters for the legitimate angler.

As we go into the 1990s the prospects for good quality roach fishing in the North West are improving all the time. As waters become cleaner, anglers better educated and tackle improved, the picture for the future is, I think, good.

The Trent

In 1962 a coach arrived out of the Manchester dawn, was boarded by some thirty men and half a dozen boys, and groaned its dirty diesel way to the Trent. The pub-punctuated journey homewards was slower still, and I had time for my thoughts that hot August night.

The walk through many meadows to my peg had been a hard one. The first barge, with its 3-foot wash, all but drowned me. My canal tackle was hopelessly inadequate for the fast current, the deep, muscular eddies and the boils of water that made a joke of a light crow's quill.

Still, I stuck to my task and, with a ten-year-old's intelligence, made enough faltering progress to land a 6oz roach. That blessed sprat of silver! It won me best roach of the day, and I was a small time hero in those bleak days . . .

As Archie Braddock explains, things have changed in a quarter of a century along the Trent . . .

Archie Braddock sets out to tackle the Trent with his usual array of exotic and experimental baits.

BETTER ROACHING AROUND THE MIDLANDS AND ALONG THE TRENT

Archie Braddock

I've fished for roach over a large slice of the Midlands for about thirty-five years, and could be forgiven for thinking I knew a bit about the roach in that area. Yet only a couple of years ago I had to start all over again, and on my local patch too.

As a teenager I fished the Trent long before its recovery from industrial pollution, and in those days roach and gudgeon were about all there was to be had, yet the roach fishing could be really good if you could sort out the better fish. Float-fished maggot brought good bags of smaller fish, with only the odd decent fish of about 8oz, but using stewed wheat was a revelation! A dozen grains were fed into the swim with every trot down and within a couple of hours you could have them almost climbing into the keepnet. They came gradually further up the swim, and higher in the water, until there was a fish for each cast within the first yard of water from the rod-tip, with the bait only 2ft deep in 8ft of water – not a roach under 6oz, with the best being 12oz. This was heady stuff in those days, and I have never lost sight of the fact that a 'big' roach is a fish that is above average for the water. Even today I would not turn my nose up at such bags, although I haven't tried wheat for years. Bearing in mind how much water the wheat absorbs while being soaked in preparation, it would be simple to flavour that water with one of today's multitude of essences, and perhaps produce a bait to end all baits. If we only had time to try everything . . .

Later on, I improved the size further still by legering: large lumps of cheese in the summer, tail-end of a lob in the winter. I caught far fewer fish, maybe five or six each time, but they were generally around 12–14oz each. Many years later, in the early 1970s, I caught more roach on legered cheese while barbel fishing. Some of these were over 1lb, with a best fish at 1lb 12oz, so the fish had obviously improved steadily as the river went through an industrial clean-up.

During the years in between, I turned to other rivers in search of chub, (the Derbyshire Derwent and Dove, the Upper Witham and Welland), and thus found some excellent roach fishing. My friends and I developed a method which we called 'follow the bread'. On a winter's day, we would start at first light at the top of a stretch perhaps a mile long and, armed with 3 or 4 stale loaves, we would feed handfuls of soaked and lightly squeezed bread in to the swim, knowing that some of it would travel quite a long way downstream. Having fished the first spot for an hour, we would move down to the next swim and repeat the process. Tactics were simple, light legering with a swan-shot link, and bread flake or crust for bait. Chub were the original target, but it was remarkable how many roach above 1lb, up to about 1lb 12oz, we caught. Also noticeable was the increase in the number and strength of bites, the lower down the stretch we progressed. This is perhaps not surprising when you consider that some of those swims would have had a steady trickle of bread particles through them for several hours.

One thing all these rivers had in common was the amount of roach bites missed. The fish seemed very fussy, especially after I'd caught a couple, often giving tiny pulls and then nothing. I turned to passing the flake down to them under a float and this worked well on some days, but with most of this fishing done in winter, low water temperatures in thick, coloured water meant that the fish wanted a static bait. It was years before I solved this problem, and the end rig is shown below. Basically I use a fixed paternoster with a 10in lead link, but a hook link of 3 or even 4ft. The bait is 'double

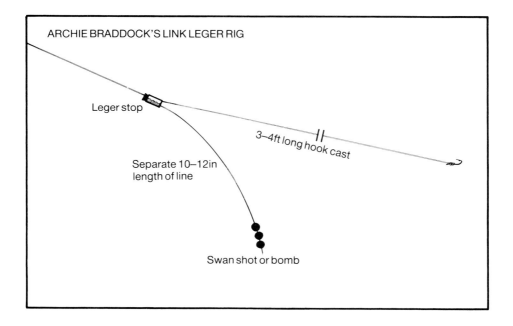

ARCHIE BRADDOCK'S LINK LEGER RIG

Leger stop

3–4ft long hook cast

Separate 10–12in
length of line

Swan shot or bomb

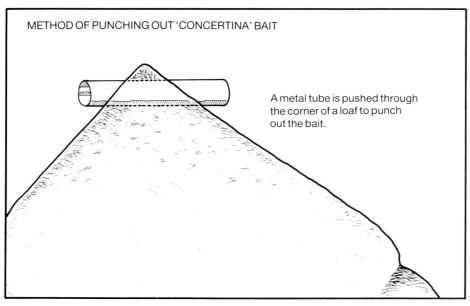

METHOD OF PUNCHING OUT 'CONCERTINA' BAIT

A metal tube is pushed through the corner of a loaf to punch out the bait.

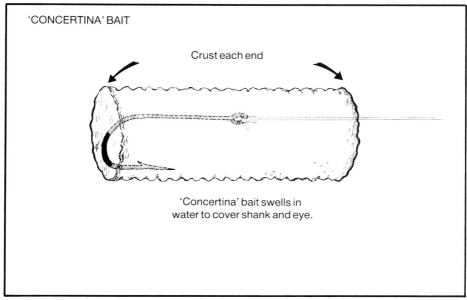

'CONCERTINA' BAIT

Crust each end

'Concertina' bait swells in water to cover shank and eye.

crust', which is produced by pushing a piece of metal tube through the corner of a loaf and extracting a concertina of flake with a crust on each end. Squeeze the concertina together to insert the long-shanked hook and, when immersed in water, the bait expands over the hook eye as in the diagram. Various sized tubes can be made from odd bits of brass, or old shotgun cartridges, for example. If you get the hook and crust sizes right, you can achieve neutral buoyancy, where the bait doesn't actually float off the bottom, but will move around on that long hook link with the slightest fluctuation of the current. The roach take the bait with confidence, as the tip moves round and keeps on going. As I was to learn later, correct presentation is vital for the bigger roach.

Along the way I did delve into canal fishing, and my first efforts on my local Erewash canal taught me what a difference fishing after dark can make on this type of water. In those days, I used a torch shining across the water on to a white-painted porcupine quill fished bottom end only, and the basic one-shot lift method. Cheese was the best bait, producing many roach over 1lb, and up to 1lb 10oz; perhaps the best example of this was when I fished the well-known Trent and Mersey Canal in the late 1970s. The water is regularly match fished, often producing nets of gudgeon and small roach. These catches come to highly skilled matchmen, using very sensitive pole tactics. My approach was a one swan waggler float, supporting a betalight, and fished hard on the bottom with a lump of cheese. There was not a flicker of a bite in the sunshine hours, with the boats proceeding up and down. Yet it was almost like a different water when the light had gone. Sailaway bites produced deep golden roach from 14oz to 1lb 4oz with often a dozen or more fish in the first hour of darkness. What a revelation that would be to those match men who line the banks weekly through the grim winter days.

Many specialist anglers feel that stillwaters offer the best chances of big roach, and at one time I felt the same. My local Staunton Harold reservoir in Derbyshire gave me quite a few roach one winter. They all fell to lobworm cast as far out as possible with a 1oz bomb. Windy days were best, and the fish seemed to need to run with the bait for at least 5–6ft, otherwise they were missed on the strike. I never got one over 1lb 8oz or less than 1lb.

Clumber Park lake in north Nottinghamshire taught me more lessons about stillwater roach than anywhere else. It is a large, stream-fed estate lake with a gravel bottom and an average depth of barely 3ft. Tactics were feeder maggot, using a streamlined feeder with a ¾oz bomb Araldited into one end. This went out like a guided missile on 3lb line, and it needed to, as the fish mainly fed in a slightly deeper area which was a long cast from the

Chris Turnbull has long known after-dark winter roaching can be productive. Here, he quivertips by torchbeam.

bank. Winter was the time to fish, as it invariably is for good roach, and the bites mostly consisted of a ¼in twitch on the betalight bobbin. I had to sit poised over the rods for an instant smash-back strike, hoping to connect with a fish perhaps 60yd away. Incredibly, these roach often would not feed until it got dark, even in bitterly cold conditions. One night in December it was dark by 5 p.m., and the lake completely froze over by 7 p.m., yet during those two hours I had more bites than ever before in the rapidly decreasing area of 3ft deep water left to me. My best fish here went up to 2lb 2oz, but anglers like Dave Plummer had fish up to 2lb 14oz.

And so to the Trent in the 1980s, where I've just *started* to learn about roach fishing. A skilful float man said to me: 'You know Arch, you'll only get these big roach on the float.' I asked him what he meant by 'big'. 'You know, those fish over two pounds,' he said. He then unfolded a story that I would not have believed, if I had not known that this angler accurately weighed his fish, and was totally reliable. It transpired that, right on my back doorstep, two or three expert float men had been quietly making the sort of roach catches most of us only dream about: 70lb of fish including five two-pounders, or a huge bag topped by seven fish in excess of 2lb, the best at 2lb 13oz. I just *knew* I could clean up with my latest feeder rigs, groundbait additives, and flavoured maggots. A year later I'd had scores of nice roach, many over the pound, but a best of only 1lb 6oz. My companion had done better, with a best of 2lb 15oz, but only the one good fish. So I went back, cap in hand, to my informant.

He unfolded to me some of the intricacies of stick float fishing, the shotting and the reasoning behind it: rates of feed, holding back, centre-pin versus fixed spool, and other points. He taught me that hook lengths were best made up and shotted at home with several identical ones ready on winders, so that vital time would not be lost once a swim had been built up. He related to me the experience of his friend, catching roach steadily in the 1lb 8oz class, while *he* could barely get them above 12oz, and told how they swapped swims, yet still his friend caught the bigger fish. A check on their apparently similar end tackles showed one tiny, but vital, difference. A number 13 shot, just 4in from the hook. Number 13? I could scarcely see the shot, never mind find the slot in it!

However, I persevered. I acquired a 13ft carbon rod, the latest light-weight fixed spool, bundles of stick floats, sinking and floating lines, stretchy line for hook links, and of course every size of split shot made. It was unfortunate that my second winter in pursuit of these Trent roach was the grim one of 1986, but I struggled to master tackle control despite the arctic conditions, and one day it all so nearly came right.

It was early February after a harsh overnight frost, and I started fishing at about 10 a.m. in comparatively cold water. I knew it would warm up, despite freezing temperatures on the bank, as the power stations came on to full load later in the day. I was tackling a medium paced glide about 7ft deep, with a small back eddy between me and the float. This gave me perfect control as the line lying on this reverse flow slowed the float's speed down just enough, compensating for my own lack of presentation. I used a 6 B.B. stick, which is heavy by most standards, but I have found it so much easier to control than lighter floats. The shots were strung out shirt-button style in the last 5ft of line, B.B. higher up, but grading right down to that number 13 about 5in from the hook. I used a 2lb reel line, 1lb 7oz hook link, and an 18 carbon whisker barb, baited with one white maggot. The river level was just dropping after being high, absolutely the right conditions for the Trent. In spite of this, it was two hours of feed and trot before the first bite, which produced a beautiful deep golden roach of exactly 1lb. The next four hours

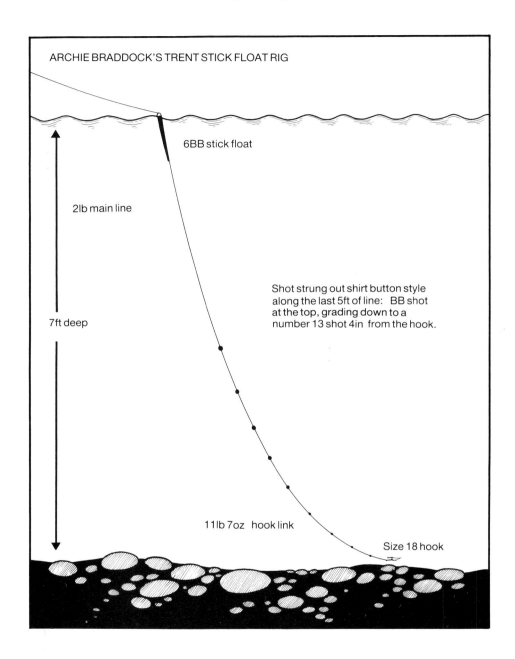

ARCHIE BRADDOCK'S TRENT STICK FLOAT RIG

6BB stick float

2lb main line

7ft deep

Shot strung out shirt button style
along the last 5ft of line: BB shot
at the top, grading down to a
number 13 shot 4in from the hook.

1lb 7oz   hook link

Size 18 hook

were half dream and half nightmare. The fish came steadily, all mint specimens, but I lost no less than three really large fish. Two came adrift during prolonged playing of them; well, I've never had roach *take line* against the clutch before. I leaned into the third one, and it promptly broke me!

Suddenly it was over. That fish had taken my last prepared hook-link, as I'd lost three others on bottom snags or bad tangles caused by faulty casting. With more than an hour of daylight left, and a swim really on the go, I frantically tried to make up a new tackle on the bank, but in the freezing conditions my fingers just wouldn't perform. A sixteen direct to 2lb line, with shots down to No. 8, was the best I could do. The fish wouldn't have it, which really emphasises the need for a correct presentation. Nevertheless, I released 31 roach back into that swim, the smallest at 14oz, the best 1lb 7oz. If only . . .

Life is full of 'if onlys', but I shall eventually get it right. This roach fishing has given a whole new zest to my angling, and has turned me into one of the strangest people in the country – I really look forward to winter!

Comment

Arranging this piece for the book led me into several telephone calls with Archie, and not one was less than marathon length. The man has so much of interest to say, I decided I really ought to visit him on this beloved river of his.

The day was nothing but good news. In a book that laments the decline of roach streams everywhere, I can only state my joy at finding the Trent – a river reborn since my last journeys to it 25 years ago. Then the river ran dirty, creamed with the soapy suds of massive effluent discharges. Anything more than a gudgeon or roach of a couple of ounces was news. Industrial society seemed to have done its worst, and no man would have fished the Trent for good fish any more than he would the moon.

This is not so today. One late summer evening in 1986, I sat on a high bank overlooking the river. Power stations were visible downstream, but across the river a church clock chimed eight and cows grazed the meadows around. As dusk began to settle, I witnessed a magic sight: all across the water, fish began to roll, big fish of all species. There were hefty bream, slightly bronzed in the last of the sun's light. Barbel head-and-shouldered like mysterious dolphins from the sea. Chub chased moths and big roach sucked at bread. Perch snapped at the heels of razor-blade skimmer bream, and somewhere, curtained out of sight by a cascade of willow, a great carp crashed through the underwater twilight. I had never seen anything like it before, never known nature so exuberant or a recovery so complete.

No man could have a better guide to the Trent than Archie Braddock. It is his river, and in the great traditions set by J.W. Martin, he understands it, loves it and has pioneered new work on it. Of particular interest is the massive experimentation being carried out with bait flavourings. His aim is to flavour particles, groundbait and hook bait, with the same overall scent and to work a swim into a frenzy of massing fish. It is fascinating that such an approach catches the biggest barbel, bream and carp, but the more careful roach stand aloof.

For them, as Archie explains in his float fishing analysis, everything has to be perfect. The heavy feeder approach is simply too clumsy for these most suspicious of big fish. It is a salutary lesson for all of us that, for the big roach, there are places and times when presentation must be accurate to the point of a needle. Such precision and sensitivity is not demanded by any other species of big fish that I know of. Barbel will suck and blow at a feeder. Carp will tolerate a 2oz bomb dropping in their feeding patch. Not so roach; a hint of clumsiness and they are away, are never caught, seen or even suspected.

There are waters where big roach do exist and where only the most delicate approach will reach them. Can any of us afford to be without a number 13 shot in future?

I do not like to go light for fear of losing fish, but have occasionally found it necessary in the past. Several instances come to mind, but one of the most striking took place on the Waveney in the mid 1970s. Some good roach had settled into a swim near the market town of Bungay. A lot of anglers knew about those fish, and the bend they were on received a good deal of attention.

On a particular Saturday in March, the pool had been fished throughout the day before I moved into it at dusk. For two hours I fished with 3lb line through to the hook and was without a bite. I knew there were roach in front of me because of their fairly frequent, heavy rolls, and I decided to go lighter: 2lb 6oz line to the hook, nothing; 1lb 7oz line, twitches; 1lb 1oz line, the bites really came at last and I took five fish to 1lb 10oz. However, like Archie, the best fish of the session, a two-pounder perhaps, broke me in a snag. I put on all the pressure I could, but in deep water with a winter push to it, a spider's web is useless with a big fish that puts its flank to the current.

Equally, in the bright, harsh, anti-cyclonic spells of winter, light lines and tiny hooks can wheedle the occasional bite from a fish that is barely inclined to feed at all. During this weather, sharp frosts kill all colour in running and

During the bright, cruel spells of winter, the lightest gear is needed.

stillwater alike and it is best to fish either very late or very light for any success at all. It is then that the type of float rig described by Archie really comes into its own.

Stillwaters

RESERVOIRS

In 1976 the *Angler's Mail* ran an embarrassing news story about my roach fishing career, entitled 'Why John turned down a place at Cambridge'.

'Dedication is a word often used to describe an angler's attitude to his sport ... but to understand what it really means you have to know the behind-the-scenes story that led to the capture of a 3lb 2oz roach from the River Wensum.

Captor John Bailey, a 25-year-old Norwich schoolteacher, is a man who was bitten by fishing early in life.

As a lad in Romiley, Cheshire, he fished the local canals and before moving to Norfolk he had a 2lb 11oz roach to his credit. Offered a place at Cambridge University, he turned it down in favour of London University, mainly because he felt that the roach fishing in London's reservoirs would offer him a greater chance of big fish.

From London he went to live and work in France for a year, following a hunch that the great European rivers would hold really massive fish. With the beginning of Norfolk's roach revival in the early 1970s, he returned to England and began teaching, because he felt that it was a job which gave him more freedom for fishing than most.'

There was a great deal of truth in that report and for some years my life had been devoted to tracking down big roach. However, the extent of the drama was a little overplayed. I was unpopular at my school for admitting the reasons for my career choice to the press, and whether I turned down Cambridge or whether that city locked its doors to me is open to debate.

What is absolutely accurate is the fact that London's reservoirs did fascinate me from the mid-1960s. Two factors had inspired me. The first was a tackle show where I had bumped into the two biggest roach I had ever seen. They were in a case and weighed 3lb 14oz and 3lb 1oz. Caught by Bill Penney in September 1938, the larger fish held the roach record for nearly forty years. (It should still. Other larger fish have been recorded, but some

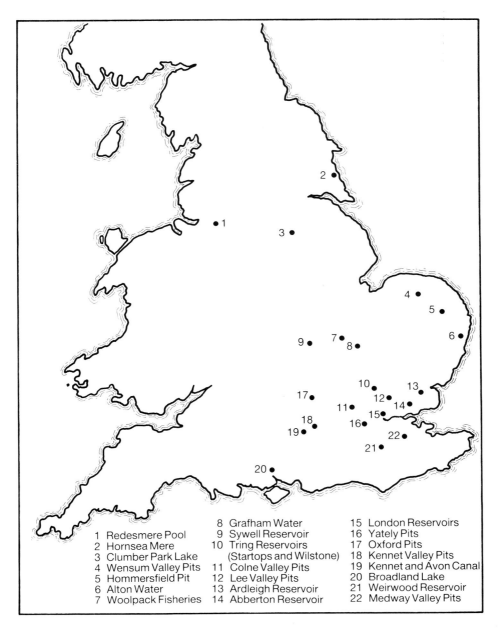

1 Redesmere Pool
2 Hornsea Mere
3 Clumber Park Lake
4 Wensum Valley Pits
5 Hommersfield Pit
6 Alton Water
7 Woolpack Fisheries
8 Grafham Water
9 Sywell Reservoir
10 Tring Reservoirs
   (Startops and Wilstone)
11 Colne Valley Pits
12 Lee Valley Pits
13 Ardleigh Reservoir
14 Abberton Reservoir
15 London Reservoirs
16 Yately Pits
17 Oxford Pits
18 Kennet Valley Pits
19 Kennet and Avon Canal
20 Broadland Lake
21 Weirwood Reservoir
22 Medway Valley Pits

Past and present big roach stillwater fisheries.

at least, like Bert Brown's 3lb 14oz fish, were hybrids. The present 4lb 1oz record contained 9oz spawn and was badly bloated. If, like the Dutch, we measured fish instead of weighing it, it would not approach Bill Penney's 18¼in long monster.)

Both these roach were caught on the same day from Lambeth Reservoir and their size and beauty quite engrossed me. Reservoirs, London reservoirs in particular then, took on a magical significance in my mind.

The second influence was a book published in 1967 by Peter Wheat called *Fishing as We Find It*. In this compilation work by specialist anglers, Peter Butler had contributed a chapter entitled 'Roach Fishing in London's Reservoirs'. The information given was detailed but, more vitally, the chapter fuelled my desire to get on reservoirs and to conquer them. Peter talked of record breaking roach there and certainly the photographs were stirring, in particular those of Peter, sporting the inevitable Richard Walker floppy hat of those days, and holding five chunky 2lb roach.

Not surprisingly, therefore, when casting around for a university, I settled for London. In my three years there I can hardly say I did well on the

Ardleigh Reservoir, near Ipswich, has produced several roach over the 3lb mark.

reservoirs, however. Good fish came my way at times but work and a social life prevented the passionate involvement I really needed.

In the 1980s, I have come back to regard reservoir roach with awe. I now fish Ardleigh reservoir near Ipswich regularly, in the autumn when the trout fishing ends, and I have seen a three-pounder from there. Even more exciting is Abberton Reservoir at Colchester. From what I have seen and from what I have been told, the future record will very possibly come from there. I do not rule out the chance of a roach nearer 5lb than 4lb . . .

Reservoir fishing obviously has huge potential for the angler seeking the better roach, and a man who has worked hard on this type of venue is Tony Miles.

RESERVOIR ROACH FISHING

by Tony Miles

When John Bailey asked me to write this chapter on reservoir roach, my first reaction was to decline graciously. The reason for this was that I felt my experience was restricted principally to one particular type of reservoir, and I have always tried to avoid the angling writer's pitfall of writing on a subject of which I have limited knowledge or experience. However, after discussing this with John, and with other anglers who are interested in reservoir roach, it appears that my water is very typical of many reservoirs up and down the country. I now know that the problems I have encountered are common, and other anglers may therefore find my experiences helpful to their own fishing, which may perhaps result in a few more roach on the bank. This section, then, is not intended to be instructional; I am not qualified for that. However, Dick Walker once said to me that all he ever hoped to achieve from his writing was to make anglers think a little more deeply about their fishing than they otherwise might have done. I could not possibly put it any better than that.

The water on which I have concentrated most of my attention in the last few winters is a typical shallow valley reservoir, dammed at one end and stream fed at the other. Like most waters of its type, it is quickly affected by any wind and, being stream fed, can rapidly colour up after rain. As the reservoir lies roughly east–west, the effects of the prevailing westerly winds are exaggerated, due to the funnelling effect of the valley. I have lost count of the days when I have left home in a pleasant breeze, but been confronted on the bank by a gale and a heavy swell. The combination of wind direction and strength, stream current speed, height, and colour, whether the stream is rising or falling, and whether water is being drawn off for any reason, such as irrigation, gives rise to endless permutations in water conditions. It also results in the very variable factor of undertow. The most fascinating, and frustrating, thing about this undertow is its total unpredictability. I have long since given up trying to understand it. I have fished pleasant, windless days, with the surface mirror smooth and the water itself crystal clear following dry weather, and yet still had to contend with a strong current below the surface. I have also fished a howling northwesterly gale, heavily coloured water from the feeder stream, with 2ft waves soaking me

A typical valley reservoir, possibly with vast roach potential.

with spray, and had no undertow at all. But most interesting of all are the countless days I've fished where there have been no appreciable changes in conditions, and yet an undertow has started, or stopped, or changed direction, for no apparent reason.

What I have established, to my own satisfaction, is that success in catching the roach consistently depends on how quickly I can determine how the feeding characteristics and location of the fish are affected by the prevailing conditions, or change in conditions. While there is no doubt that roach are very much like carp in the way in which they respond to wind strength and direction, I'm convinced that the presence of a sub-surface current is the most critical factor. Find an undertow, and you've found roach.

These days, my swim selection is based on the conditions that greet me on my arrival. In which direction is the wind, and how strong? Which area of the lake is most affected by the chop? If the water is coloured, is it a general condition, or is the colouring localised? I have found that the onset of colouring, with the stream rising following heavy rain, can drive the roach crazy. Once I have established the general area I feel should be the most productive, I will then cast around with an empty swim feeder to see if I can locate an undertow, sometimes testing several hundred yards of bank, if angling pressure allows. Once I have located an undertow, or have established that it is stronger in one particular area, I will fish there. I would sum up the perfect conditions for reservoir roach as a mild, overcast day, following heavy rain which has produced coloured water, with a good chop and a steady undertow. I would be very confident of catching roach under these circumstances.

The importance of locating an undertow was brought home to me quite forcibly three years ago. I had arrived at the water at dawn, and was pleased to find what appeared to be perfect conditions, with a mild, moderate northeasterly ruffling the surface invitingly. The swims towards the lower end of the west bank looked particularly promising, as they were getting the maximum effect of the breeze. These swims are, in fact, well-known roach producing areas, and I was happy to settle into one of these and start fishing. A couple of biteless hours later, I was joined by my old mate Merv Wilkinson, and after a short chat he set up shop about 200yd further up the reservoir. Not a sign of a bite had I seen, when I stopped fishing at about midday for a short while, and strolled up the bank for a talk to Merv. I was interested to learn that he had had a couple of nice roach, with several bites missed. I was more interested to notice several spirals of lead wire around his butt indicators. I mentioned this, and Merv said that despite the lead wire, the indicators had still been creeping upwards with the undertow; it had got so bad that he had had to change his feeder for a ¾oz bomb. This was amazing. Only 200yd away, in identical conditions, I had no undertow at all! In the short space of time I stood there, Merv had a further three bites, two half-hearted affairs that he missed, and a pronounced drop back that produced a spanking roach of exactly 2lb. Back at my own tackle, I confirmed the absence of undertow by several trial casts in the vicinity, and then decided to stay put so that Merv and I could compare notes in the evening. Despite fishing very hard, I never had a sign of a bite all day, while Merv had several more roach, and many missed bites. When I analysed these facts, I felt that it was all down to the undertow. I was fishing a well-proven roach swim, and although I may not be as good a roach angler as Merv (more than a distinct possibility), I am certainly competent enough to get a few bites if fish are present. No, the fish simply were not there. There is no doubt in my mind that the roach knew where the current was, and sought it out in preference to other areas.

If the prevailing conditions can, at times, give a clue to the all-important location of the fish, they can also lead to wide variations in feeding behaviour. The very common problem of missed bites can be attributed to this variation, from which we all suffer. In my first winter on the reservoir, when I was trying to come to terms with the fishing, it is no exaggeration to say that I was probably missing two out of every three bites I had. I will never forget one particular two-day session. On the Friday, which was a very calm day, I had just four confident bites, with the bobbin sailing up to

Large roach like this can be highly mobile, sensitive to any change in their environment.

the butt ring. Each bite resulted in a good roach, hooked well back in the mouth. The following day, with a good wind on the water, I had about twenty identical bites, which resulted in the grand total of one roach! Needless to say, this was a highly unsatisfactory state of affairs, and I came to the conclusion, so obvious in hindsight, that my approach to the fishing had become far too stereotyped. I had become too content to sit behind a pair of feeder rods, always using the same terminal rig of a running feeder with an 18in tail, which had served me so well in the past. My results clearly showed that an effective terminal rig was rendered nearly useless by a change in conditions. I determined that on my next session I would respond to a missed bite by trying to analyse why I had missed it, and alter my terminal tackle accordingly. My next two-day session was to prove fascinating, and I would like to repeat here a section of an article of mine that first appeared in *Specialist Angler*. I make no apology for repeating it, as the lessons I learned from that session have stood me in good stead ever since.

'On the first day, I started off a little after dawn in a swim I knew well, having caught good roach from it on previous occasions. It was a mild, sunny day, and when I started fishing, a gentle breeze was blowing directly into my bank. By mid-morning, the breeze had become quite a strong wind and fishing was uncomfortable. I had started with my normal twin feeder rods, using running Drennan feeders and an 18in, 2lb hook length. On one, tackle was a 16 hook baited with two flavoured white maggots, and on the other an 18 baited with a single pinkie. The bite detection method was butt mounted bobbins, with an 18in drop.

Almost immediately, before the wind had picked up, I had a sharp ½in lift on one bobbin. This happened twice more in the next few minutes, and on the third occasion I tried a strike. I felt nothing, but on winding in found I had smashed maggots. This obviously told me that the bait had been well inside the fish's mouth, and as I had very little indication, I reduced the tail length to 6in. During the next hour, I had two more bites very similar to the first, and with exactly the same result. So I tried a dodge I had used successfully during my summer tench fishing: 3in above the feeder I pinched on a swan shot, effectively converting the terminal arrangement into a version of the shock rig. For the next half-hour that worked like a dream. I had two bites which produced roach of 1lb 6oz and 1lb 11oz. The bites were identical. I had the initial twitch I had come to expect, and then the bobbin rocketed to the butt. What was happening, of course, was that as the fish was twitching the bait, the swan shot jammed behind the feeder, causing the roach to bolt. Result: two very positive bites.

At about 11 a.m., there was a change in the conditions. As well as the steadily increasing wind strength, an undertow started. By 1 p.m., the tow was very heavy and the bobbins were creeping upwards constantly. To combat this, and as I was now expecting good bites, I put the line in clips. Nothing happened then until 3 p.m. when, upon winding in to rebait, I was attached to a roach of 1lb 9oz. I had not seen a bite. At first I put this down to one of those things, but in the next hour I wound in three times to find my bait smashed without seeing any indication whatever. It appeared that the roach were no longer prepared to tolerate resistance. Consequently, I removed the clips, counteracting the tow with swan shot on the bobbins instead, and removed the shot from behind the feeder, reverting to the sliding rig. Leaving the tail length at 6in, I rebaited and cast out. Within five minutes, I had a lovely bite, with the bobbin running steadily up to the butt. I missed it, and the maggots appeared untouched, indicating that I had struck too early. Accordingly, I increased the tail length to 18in – I was now back where I started. Another immediate bite was missed in the same way, so I doubled the tail to 3ft. This did the trick. In my remaining time I had six more bites, resulting in five roach and a bonus bream of 7lb 10oz as darkness fell. All the fish were hooked well back in the mouth. During the drive home, my thoughts were occupied with the tackle modifications I had employed to put a few fish on the bank. It was also interesting how the

Dave Phillips with a superb 2lb 12oz fish from an East Anglian lake.

frequency of the bites had increased with the stronger wind and the onset of the undertow.

When I arrived just after first light the next morning, it was obvious that the wind was very much stronger than on the previous day. As it was also raining heavily, it would make the same swim very unpleasant. I therefore elected to fish from a spot a little further round the reservoir, where I could fish with the wind coming from my left, and therefore from the comfort of my umbrella. I had given the previous day's events some considerable thought, and had decided to fish with one rod only, with either a swingtip or quivertip as bite indicator, depending on wind strength. I wanted to hold the rod all day so that I could be in as good a position as possible to assess what was going on at the business end. I started off with the same terminal rig with which I had finished the previous evening, with a 3ft tail. I began using a swingtip indicator, but because of the high bank, the gale force wind and the strong undertow, the tip was flapping around uncontrollably, even with lead wire around it. I therefore changed to a 2½oz Drennan quivertip. I very quickly had a good pull on the tip, just like a chub bite, but I missed completely. The maggots were untouched, so I increased the tail to 5ft. For the rest of that day I had no further need to alter my terminal tackle. I had seven more bites, all very positive pulls, which resulted in seven well-conditioned roach of between 1lb 4oz and 1lb 15oz.'

The lessons I learned in those two days, which I freely admit are largely common sense, have changed my approach to reservoir roaching. Having now fished for them through most winter conditions, and having made careful notes of my observations during each trip, I am now more consistently able to select the correct terminal arrangement to suit the conditions with which I am faced. Although missed bites still occur of course, they now form a very small percentage, and as such are a minor irritation when compared with the major frustration they used to be.

In these days of matched rods and Optonics, I have found the use of one rod with quivertip or swingtip for reservoir roach a refreshing change, and extremely enjoyable. I have even caught a couple touch legering. I suppose in some ways it reminds me of chub fishing, with which I was brought up. I certainly get more of a feeling of being involved with the fishing if I am holding the rod. I am not saying that it is more effective, because, generally speaking, I am sure that it is not. It all comes down to personal preference. At present I fish both ways, to suit whatever my mood may be. If I have had a particularly stressful week at the office, I may fancy lolling lazily behind two rods, taking the opportunity to wind down completely. In this mood, I can occasionally allow my attention to wander to the sights and sounds of the countryside, knowing that the Optonic will alert me to the business in hand at the required moment. Alternatively, I may be in a more determined frame of mind, and sit holding a quivertip rod with absolute concentration for hour after hour, not missing a single movement. Both are enjoyable in their different ways, and, of course, enjoyment should be what it is all about.

Having said all that, there are two circumstances where I feel that the use of one rod with a tip indicator may have the edge. These circumstances are the extremes in conditions. Firstly, there is the flat calm day with not a ripple in sight, bright winter sunshine, clear water and no undertow. I have found these conditions the most difficult, but I have managed to pick up quite a few fish on the swingtip, using fixed feeders, short tails, and striking at small movements. The same bites can often not be taken on the Optonic/bobbin set up. Secondly, there is the exact opposite, the howling gale coupled with an undertow so strong that it causes the heaviest bobbin to rise continually. In these circumstances, I like to fish the quivertip, with the feeder lead-loaded to such an extent that the tip can be bent into the lead at a substantial curve, before dislodging it. With this combination adjusted correctly, so that the feeder does not roll with the undertow, conditions are then similar to those of upstream legering for chub or barbel. Because the tackle is quite finely balanced, even a small pull will dislodge it, releasing the tension in the tackle, and resulting in an unmissable spring back on the tip. Obviously, a similar effect can be obtained by substituting a heavily loaded butt indicator for the quivertip, the bite then being signalled by the indicator dropping to the floor.

One of the most interesting days I have ever spent at my reservoir was when I was fishing in this way three years ago, and sat for most of the day in driving snow. The north wind was so strong that the snow was horizontal, and the water more closely resembled the North Sea than a peaceful English reservoir. I had the water to myself, which was hardly surprising. I cannot

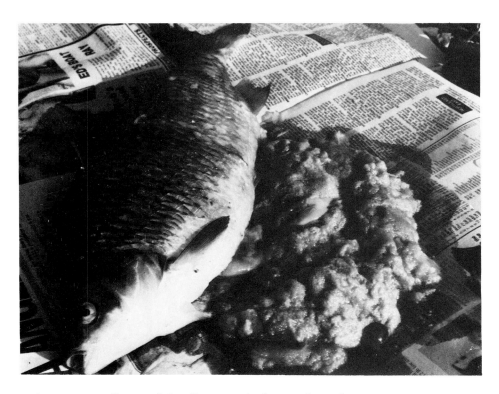

A fascinating stillwater fish, 3lb 1oz. It died spawnbound, laden with 9½oz of eggs.

recall ever feeling so cold in my life, but I could not pack up, so engrossed was I in the fishing. I was at the water at first light, and straight away went on to my stiffest quivertip, fished as close to the water's surface as possible, to minimise the effect of the wind. The undertow was fantastic – I've never experienced one stronger. Eventually, with about 1oz lead on the feeder, I had the tackle balanced so that the tip could be bent into a quarter circle before dislodging the end rig. I was not expecting finicky bites that day, and I would not have seen one if I'd had one in such wild conditions. In the light of previous experiences, I used a 3ft tail with a running feeder. At about mid-morning, with the wind getting wilder and the snow more persistent, I was asking myself serious questions concerning my sanity. Suddenly, the tip sprang back, I struck immediately, and felt a resistance on the end for a second or two before I pulled out. A second identical bite about fifteen minutes later was missed completely, and that was my signal to increase the tail to 5ft. Thereafter there were no more problems. In the next hour or so I had three more bites which yielded roach of 1lb 9oz, 1lb 14oz, and 2lb 1oz. The bite indications were unmistakable, even in those wild conditions. The rod really lurched back in my hand as the tension went out of the tackle. At about midday, the undertow stopped suddenly, even though the wind was, if anything, getting stronger – and I do mean *suddenly*. One minute there was a very strong tow, the next minute, nothing. I could not explain it then, and I cannot now. But, whatever the reason, it signalled the end of the bites, and when I packed up four hours later I had not had another touch.

Having discussed the vitally important areas of location and correct bait presentation, I feel that the actual hook bait choice is not so critical. I have had reservoir roach on maggots, casters, flake, crust, sweetcorn, redworms, lobworms, and trout pellet paste, although most of the fish have fallen to maggots. What I am finding, though, is that flavoured maggots seem to take more fish than plain ones. Over several weeks, I fished two identical rigs side by side, one using maggots flavoured with 'roach attractor' (which sounds quite logical) and the other using natural maggots. Although I will say right away that the number of fish caught over that period was probably too small for an accurate statistical analysis, the results, for what they are worth, show a four to one preference for flavoured bait. I now add flavourings to my maggots all the time, the ones that I have caught most on being 'roach attractor', pineapple and strawberry. Whatever else they may do, they give me confidence, and that is always an important consideration.

Far more important than the hook bait is thoughtful groundbaiting. My results, and those of many friends and acquaintances on several similar reservoirs, show that it is very easy to overdo the groundbaiting.

Pre-baiting, and heavy baiting on the day, have yielded generally very poor results. It is important to realise here that I am talking about *big* roach. On my particular reservoir, heavy baiting has produced hordes of tiny roach, hybrids, bream and plagues of jack pike. It certainly seems, from my experience, that the old 'little and often' principle is the most effective approach for big reservoir roach. What I currently use is an inverted Drennan feeder, fished open at the bottom, and plugged with groundbait. I generally make half a dozen casts to start, to put a little bait in the swim, and then content myself with topping up by recasting my baits periodically. Most of the successful anglers with the big roach of Startops adopt the same principle.

The 'little and often' principle only works effectively if the introduction of the bait is accurate, and I feel it vitally important that I should go to the trouble to hit the same spot every time. The simplest, and most effective method I know is to cast out to the required spot, and then encircle the spool with insulating tape. Taking up the slack then puts a few turns of line on the tape. On every subsequent cast the tape halts the terminal tackle over the same spot, assuming the direction is accurate.

As with the flavoured hookbaits, I have had good results with various combinations of flavoured and coloured groundbaits. It is always difficult, of course, to establish whether I have caught because of the groundbait, or whether I would have caught just as well on plain breadcrumb. However, messing about with different baits is good fun. One of my favourite combinations is fine bread crumb, trout fry crumb, and finely ground rusk, to make the bait 'explode', all coloured yellow. I am not at all sure whether the colouring makes any difference, but it certainly doesn't seem to have had a detrimental effect. I have certainly established to my own satisfaction that the yellow coloration is an attractant to gravel pit tench.

There you have it then, an outline of what I consider to be the more important observations I have been able to make in the last few winters of reservoir roaching. By no stretch of the imagination would I call myself an expert, but a few things are starting to come together. One thing is for certain: reservoir fishing for big roach is a fascinating and thoroughly absorbing branch of angling.

Comment

What Tony says about undertow bears direct comparison with my experience on the larger pits I have fished for roach. There too the shoals seem to follow the underwater currents, I suppose for the food they bring or disturb,

My most unusual, not to say repulsive, roach bait was congealed blood.

and keep well clear of slack areas. Like Tony, I cannot offer any explanation for the unpredictability of undertows. To me they seem to have a mind of their own and to fit no simple theories.

It is as well not to go to any big stillwater, pit or reservoir, with a preconceived idea of where to fish and, as Tony says, searching with an empty swim feeder can locate the channels of water with the strong movement. Fish there. That is where the roach are. Did I say pits and reservoirs are 'stillwaters'? Nothing could be further from the truth. On the big waters, roach probably fight current speeds more strongly than in a slow moving river.

Tony's understanding and use of terminal gear and bite indication are masterly. What he reveals is the subtlety of these absorbing fish and the certainty that the stereotyped angler will miss out. He is equally inventive and pioneering with flavoured baits.

As you have read, Archie Braddock is experimenting with flavours on the Trent with very promising results. My own trials have centred around bread baits scented with carp attractors. For me, results were inconclusive

*It flowed into Ireland's Blackwater River from the
slaughtered pigs at the Cappoquin Bacon Factory.*

and I moved to the commercially available roach attractors.

I still remain unconvinced. My big roach are lightly, if ever, fished for, and many have never seen a bait. Suspicion is not therefore a factor as it might be with the very wise Trent fish, who have seen most tricks in this or any other book!

Flavouring did, however, winkle out a couple of fish for me in the very cold weather of February 1986 when normal baits remained untouched. It could be that the dash of attractor does prove a stimulus in these extreme conditions and is worth further trials.

PITS AND LAKES

I do roach fish pits and lakes. If you want big fish constantly, you must attack the stillwaters, but certainly I, and all the other roach men I have known, prefer rivers. Just as carp, bream and tench are stillwater fish, so roach are real river dwellers. True roaching is river fishing; that is where the art and the soul of the sport is to be found.

Having made that clear, in this chapter I want to do two things: firstly, swiftly, I would like to pass on my approach to pit and lake roach; secondly, more vitally I believe, I would like to look at what makes a big roach stillwater. I will be taking up the points that David Carl Forbes made in *Successful Roach Fishing*, but adding to them the thoughts generated in the near fifteen years since that book was published.

I would be pressed to improve upon Tony Miles's assessment of terminal rigs and bite indication in large stillwaters. I agree with everything he says, and can only build around his points for this first section.

To fish pits or lakes successfully, I really believe you must get out there on them with a boat, to obtain a precise idea of the contours. Bankside plumbing is slow and inaccurate; a day on the bank teaches you less than an hour in a boat. Conventional depth finding is so much easier this way, but, if you can obtain a graph recorder, the preparation is bliss. Recently, Roger Miller and I had access to just such a machine, and in a two hour period, we accurately charted a twenty-four acre gravel pit. From the bank such accuracy would have been impossible, and what we could have managed would have taken two weeks at least.

Boats have an added advantage. It was Alastair Nicholson who alerted me to the possibility of spotting fish at night with a powerful torch beam played into the water. For Alastair, this has worked with carp and bream. Since then, it has shown up good roach for me.

Roach shoals on large pits and lakes are not static. Under many conditions, I believe they are almost continually on the move, very much like a bream shoal. Unlike bream, however, roach are not usually as visible and their patrol routes are less easy to plot. For this reason, when I am afloat, depth recording, I am looking for the type of areas I know bigger roach like to frequent.

I am constantly looking for large plateau-like areas that can be 2–8ft deep. These might not be totally flat, and often slope gently towards deeper

A roach fractionally under 2lb, ambushed from a gravel bar.

water. If they are close enough to the bank to be fished comfortably, I am excited. If they are towards the north and east of a water, where the frequent southwesterlies really build up over them, I am very excited. Roach, like carp, follow the wind on large stillwaters and if a force 5 or 6 has been blowing for some hours, any roach are likely to be feeding there in front of it.

Again, like a carp man, I like to plot the network of gullies every pit contains. Most lakes, too, have deeper central channels where the original stream carved out its bed. Roach shoals obviously follow these contours and, where gravel bars meet up and cross, an excellent ambush point presents itself. I prefer a gravel bar to be not too steep sided, and I aim to put bait on gravel or a hard bottom rather than over deep silt.

Finally, I always make some note of areas of deeper water. These holes will be in the 12–22ft range and they might well hold fish in cold, high pressure periods during December, January and February when the roach gravitate towards darker, warmer surroundings.

So, I come inevitably to fishing conditions for these waters. I begin on them in September and go through until March. The best stillwaters clear out almost completely in the autumn and winter, and to fish them in strong light is useless. I rarely settle down before sundown and will fish well into darkness. Midnight is not too late to pick up big roach even well into December when some fish seem to become totally nocturnal.

Obviously, I prefer the wet, mild, windy nights when I know big fish will be on the move, actively feeding. Then I can fish with some confidence and 'liners' can often show within the first minutes of setting up. However, I also realise that, no matter how still and cold the night becomes, there is always a chance of a roach as the night progresses. All I can say is that it does take true grit to be out on a pit towards midnight as the frost crackles around you. As an incentive, such a session often does produce the very biggest fish – even if only one or two bites can be expected. Keep warm, and keep interested. In temperatures well below freezing, a bite can be very shy.

My gear is simple and I have not thought as deeply about it as Tony so obviously has. I prefer a feederlink to all other tools and, like Archie Braddock, often use the Araldited bomb if extreme range is necessary. As a pretty constant rule, I avoid cereal groundbait and so the feederlink with a maggot/hemp mix is perfect for my approach. Maggot and hemp in the feeder does not preclude the use of bread on the hook. Indeed, I believe a piece of flake is often the first morsel to be picked up by what can be the best fish. Like everybody else, I like to think that I am fishing tight to my chosen feature. This is always my aim, but in the pitch darkness of a November gale, I cannot guarantee that I do not spread the feed around a fair area. At least, in such conditions, I can feel confident that the fish are active, very busily looking for food and my confidence remains high.

It was on just such a night, when I felt that I was fishing abysmally, that I recorded my best ever bag of pit roach. In three hours I took 27 fish for over 40lb, when I was averaging less than a roach each session. I could do nothing wrong. The slightly coloured, highly oxygenated water seemed to mask my every mistake to give me an eternal highlight.

I do not think pit and lake roach are particularly difficult to catch. Preparation, dedication and sensible fishing will see roach come to the net. It is harder, in my view, to find the stillwaters where big roach actually exist. In 1975–1976, when I began large stillwater fishing seriously, it took me 27 pits before I clicked with big roach. They do not exist everywhere. Whether pit, lake or reservoir, you cannot guarantee that roach of 1lb 8oz or more are present. Some waters go through cycles, and their roach are on the decline. Others never have the capacity to produce large specimens. We now move on to what David Carl Forbes called, in 1973, his 'Environmental Theory'.

A very fine 2lb 6oz fish that fought well and did not seem to suffer from its affliction with black spot.

He explained how the once famous London reservoirs, Hornsea Mere in Yorkshire and the Broads of Norfolk had all fallen on hard times as far as roach over 2lb were concerned. He suggested that waters have a limited 'climax of fertility' that can produce huge roach, but this is transitory. He believed that roach waters 'wear out' – rather like an overcropped field or an overtired body.

At the time that the book was published, I had considerable sympathy with this idea and since then this has increased. My experiences since 1975 lead me to believe that the newest of pits are almost invariably those most capable of producing very big roach. I have found that pits often reach a climax at around 8–15 years of age, and though they do not produce large numbers of roach, these first settlers can grow very large.

Why this is, I can only guess. Perhaps the secret lies in the vitality of new pits. Food is rich and in David Carl Forbes's phrase 'the water is building up to a climax of fertility'. Perhaps the lack of competition in these new waters is important. The original roach are almost alone there. The best food is theirs to pick and choose from, and their growth rate reflects this. In addition, their spawning is inhibited by the lack of weed, reed and silt in a new pit. The wind whips across new waters and keeps the temperatures low, often too low for eggs to hatch or for fry to survive. Whilst the fledgling population struggles, the stock of pioneering fish grow on to huge size. My one 3lb stillwater roach came from just such an environment: ten years on I would not like to bet on even two-pounders being present, now that the roach stock has expanded greatly.

I find the discovery period on a new pit gripping. Angling is as much about anticipation as anything else and my dreams always run to three- and even four-pounders when I look out over vast, near virgin waters. It is just as well they do – the fishing can be diabolically difficult for a very few, very well fed roach. Stocks may not exceed three to five roach per acre and you have got to be a believer . . .

Such stillwater excitement is not restricted to pits. Lakes can produce the same type of fever in me. However, with them I find that a period of big roach follows some type of ecological upheaval. Let me give some examples.

Gunton Park Lake in Norfolk produced this 2lb roach for John Nunn, float fishing from a boat.

*An old-established lake which has begun to produce big roach
as chemical infiltration has upset its environmental balance.*

Gunton Lake in Norfolk is around a dozen acres. Through the 1960s it
teemed with small roach until the then River Board netted it extensively and
removed the vast majority of them. For some years, the roach population
lay low, until quite by chance bream fishing, friends and I stumbled on to
superb fish of 2lb and more. Obviously the few roach remaining had done
well when 98 per cent of their fellows had been removed, and we reaped the
benefit for a few years.

More permanent damage than netting or simple disease is being done to
certain old established lakes in the heavily farmed areas of England. Many
of these, especially those in estates, act as sinks or soak-aways to large areas
of crop land. Since the chemical fertilizer revolution in agriculture of the
1960s, vast amounts of often conflicting chemicals have drained into these
lakes and upset the environmental balance. I have no doubt that tench, rudd
and roach find their fry are unable to survive and normal regeneration
breaks down. These lakes are, in a very real sense, in their death throes.

However, in the five to ten years before they perish absolutely, the
surviving roach can put on a great deal of weight. As their numbers

dwindle, so their average size increases from a few ounces to a pound and from several ounces to even two pounds or more. Such a situation is obviously not desirable; it is tragic, but we can at least exploit it and benefit while we can. The sunset can be outstandingly golden.

So, whilst the fluctuating fortunes of our river roach tend to receive the greatest publicity, never think that the populations of pits, lakes and reservoirs remain static. They do not. The man who wants big stillwater roach must be aware of the environment's dynamics, and catch his fish on either their 'ups' or their 'downs'. David Carl Forbes's 'Environmental Theory' is, as far as I am concerned, fact.

East Anglian Rivers

I came to the Norfolk rivers very much by design. My parents retired to the county and so from the mid 1960s I was fishing there in earnest. In 1973, I made the decision to settle there full time. As a schoolmaster, I realised that East Anglia would be unlikely to offer me great scope or variety – but when fishing is all important, life is far more than work.

Today, I find it all but impossible to describe how magnificent the roach fishing in the Wensum, Yare, Bure and Waveney could be, right until the late 1970s. Since then, many younger specialist anglers have come into the sport and just cannot imagine how things were in the glory days of ten, fifteen and twenty years ago. Perhaps it would be best to retell a sample of old memories and diary jottings, to give some clue to what a roaching life was like then.

Lyng: River Wensum, August 1972. I arrived at dawn and pushed a way through the loosestrife and nettles still damp with the dew. The river ran clear and full of weed. Until sun-up I legered into a clear hole with little success. Now fresh light falling on to the water changed all that. At once I could see fish lying not on the bottom, as I had expected, but in midwater and above. Some of them – not a few but literally hundreds – were actually just sub-surface, their red fins breaking the film, catching the sunbeams. And very many of these were big fish . . .

I threw in a dozen slices of mashed flake, some to sink slowly, some to float and, within five yards, the whole amount had been attacked and consumed. A freelined crust at once took a roach a shade under 2lb. So it went on, as the sun climbed higher towards noon. All that morning I took roach, perhaps seventy to eighty in all. Eight were two-pounders. The largest was 2lb 9oz. The shoal itself, made up of fish from 1lb to nearly 3lb, must have numbered not less than two thousand roach, and probably a lot more.

The Wensum again, this time in winter: December 1975 through to March 1976, a period when I fished hard and was only driven off the river by a terrible February, when even midday temperatures were consistently below freezing. I was looking for still larger fish – the big two-pounders – and perhaps even my first clear three-pounder. (I had taken half a dozen fish

The ultimate reward of the roaching life! A perfectly formed Norfolk fish, only ounces off 3lb.

over 2lb 15oz, nudging 3lb, but now I was on the trail of a fish quite distinctly over 3lb.)

My decision had been made to concentrate on the areas of river where populations were low in the assumption that what fish there were would be large ones.

The turn of 1976 was gruelling. In all, I recorded 33 blank sessions — many day long, from dawn to two or three hours after sunset. The weather, almost throughout, was atrocious. I did not have a bite. I did not see a single fish. Yet I believed there would be reward if I could be dogged enough to see the hunt through.

We move into January. We are nearing the end of that 34th session, a 12-hour affair that had begun at 6 a.m. and had dragged on well after dark. A wind had sprung up from the west during the afternoon and, by twilight, it was gusting towards gale. Watching a bobbin was a nightmare of a job, but in one of the lulls, I had a suspicion, no more, of a slight drop back bite. I reached down and struck out of hope alone. When the rod had gone far back, I connected.

*Chris Turnbull's impression of Wensum fishing that terrible
February.*

The fruits of that fabulous period – two marvellous fish of 2lb 11oz and 2lb 14oz.

That roach again weighed 2lb 15oz and confirmed my feeling for the swim, for the stretch, for everything that I was doing. In the thirteen sessions that followed, I took another fourteen fish. Only one was below 2lb 10oz, at 2lb 4oz. The average weight of the fourteen was 2lb 14oz. The largest weighed 3lb 2oz and I lost a fish at the very net that could not have weighed less than 3lb 8oz. In short, it was the best fishing for massive roach I have ever known.

Let me now move on to the River Yare, in 1975, low down near Norwich, where it runs slowly and meanders towards the outer suburbs. I was catching fish at dusk there after work. They were good roach, up to 2lb 7oz, but they only came erratically in ones and twos. I never had a bag of fish and I came to believe that stocks were low. Not until a certain November night did I realise how many fish were in the stretch.

What was different about that particular dusk, I will never know. It was unusually warm for the month, almost muggy with a low cloud cover, but I feel sure a deeper reason prevailed. Perhaps some strange insect hatched out

*Probably the most valued roach of my life – 3lb 2oz and,
then, the Wensum record.*

that night to draw the roach up, but all I can say with conviction is that the
stretch of river I was fishing came alive with fish.

For half a mile, the river was constantly pock-marked by the rings of
heavily rising fish. For two hours the activity continued. Each minute saw
hundreds of fish top, and when the full moon rode high, I began to see
individual roach clearly. Their sides gleamed in the new light and glittered
like stardust thrown on the river. Not many of these hundreds of fish were
less than two pounds and some were larger than I had ever caught there.

The appearance of the moon, however, signalled the break up of the
cloud and the dropping of the temperature. The fish showed less and less
until, by 9 p.m., the whole event might never have occurred. But I, and
Sharon with me that night, will both remember it for ever.

Why the 1970s produced such sights and sessions as those described
above, we can never be quite sure. Most probably the answer lies in a
combination of circumstances. All were very rich rivers at that time. Snails,
caddis, bloodworm, shrimp – all foods were present in huge quantities.

For generations, centuries probably, the food stocks and water quality
had produced big-bodied roach, deep-sided, thick-set fish that weighed
very heavy for their length. A 12½in, 2lb fish was always a possibility and,

Those marvellous East Anglian days when, with so many
roach, the otters could thrive.

The tell-tale signs of columnaris, *the disease which decimated East Anglian roach stocks.*

when the length potential was 18 and 19in, huge fish of 3–4lb were always more than a dream.

The 1970s were also the boom decade in a natural roach cycle. During the 1960s, roach of all sizes had proliferated throughout the river, in shoals hundreds of yards long. Many were good fish, but few reached 2lb, so they were, if you like, stunted even at 1lb–1lb 12oz. In the late 1960s, however, the roach disease *columnaris* struck the rivers. I know most about its effect on the Wensum.

Rapidly ulcerated sores began to appear on the roach, pushing away the scales, exposing the red raw flesh. Death generally followed and estimates are that 90 per cent of the Wensum roach stocks present in 1966 had perished by 1969.

Survivors were still numerous, compared with the 1980s, but throughout the 1970s, they obviously benefited from the lack of competition for food stocks. By 1973–74, it was apparent that growth rates had rocketed. 2lb fish were common and the very big two-pounders – perhaps 2lb 12oz and above – were making their appearances.

63

A close-up of survivors from the disease; fish still badly scarred.

Many of these fish were not pristine roach by any standards. *Columnaris* had, literally, scarred them for life. My first 'super' fish of 2lb 13oz had, instead of a dorsal fin, a great purple/red gash along the top of its back. Scale formations were often jumbled and sores still persisted. Gill covers were eaten away. Blindness was not uncommon in one, and sometimes in both eyes. Fins were frequently absent – one memorable roach only possessed three out of the customary seven.

Even today in the late 1980s, big fish still show signs of the disease. Whether these are old scars, or whether the virus is still active in the rivers, no one is yet sure. It is possible that *columnaris* has contributed to the decline of the fish stocks that we are now seeing in 1986–87. Certainly, since 1978, the roach fishing that peaked in 1973–77, has become very hard indeed. Many blank sessions must be expected on all the rivers. Whole stretches of Wensum, Bure, Yare and Waveney, have lost their *entire* roach stocks, and everywhere a lot of searching and trial fishing must be undertaken.

*This huge Wensum roach, 3lb 10oz, could at certain times of
the year threaten the British record.*

Just as the success of the rivers was due to a combination of factors, so are their difficulties today. The residual effect of *columnaris* could play a part. A too fast run off from the mills in the winter, I believe, has resulted in fry and small fish being swept gradually from the higher reaches to the lower.

Above all, of course, the growth in chemical drainage from the arable lands of East Anglia has devastated the once stable river environment. Nitrates, fungicides, pesticides have all mixed to produce potentially lethal cocktails for young fish and fry.

Nor, of course, have frequent pollutions helped this situation. Anglian Water itself has the worst record on the Wensum – its Fakenham sewage works have broken down repeatedly, and in 1976 250,000 gallons of raw sewage made its way down the low summer river.

Are the rivers of East Anglia worth fishing today? The answer, I fear, is a delicate one. Certainly there are still present, in the Wensum particularly, a few huge fish – some that could nudge the British record. For the true specialist angler, therefore, the rewards are potentially enormous, even if the work involved is appalling to contemplate.

Beneath these pinnacle roach, there are stretches on all the rivers where good fish can indeed be caught – sometimes in reasonable numbers. Areas of the Upper Bure are making particularly strong recoveries. John Nunn, for example, has had a three-pounder in the 1980s and many fine back-up fish.

The 1990s are in doubt, but I do feel there is some case for cautious optimism. Like rabbits and myxomatosis, it is possible that the roach will learn to live with modern agricultural chemicals and even flourish again. This has happened in the Lincolnshire Wolds. In the drains of that heavily farmed area, roach all but vanished in the 1970s. They are now making a strong and sure come back, despite continued run offs. Certainly, if nature is easily knocked down, she can also be very quick to pick herself up again. Take the Glaven as an example – this tiny river that runs into the sea off the north Norfolk coast was once a roach haven. Then a trout farm was built, and within two years the roach stocks fell into decline. The quality of the weed decreased and food stocks were decimated. For the following decade, roach all but vanished with just a few fish maintaining a precarious presence in the river.

Two years ago, the trout farm closed. Almost at once the remaining roach spawned. The weed recovered and gave both food and shelter to the fry. A few weeks ago I counted twenty different shoals of roach, averaging thirty fish in each, with individuals reaching the 10–12oz mark. There is every indication that within three or four years, the Glaven could again be the

John Nunn admires his breathtaking 3lb 3oz Bure fish.

roach river it was twenty years ago. If only rivers could be given more chances of this sort, then I do believe we might again see the roaching of the past.

AN APPROACH
TO EAST ANGLIAN RIVERS

At certain points of this discussion I have brought in Roger Miller; I do this because he is younger than me, a little, and did not know the rivers in their heyday, but has come later on to the scene without preconceived ideas. He has worked hard on the waters that are more difficult today, and he has done well. In addition, he has probably greater experience on the Bure and the Waveney than I have. A Suffolk lad, he was born on the Waveney, and he now lives in Norfolk, on the Bure – a very unpredictable river indeed, and one that reacts to certain conditions quite unlike the Wensum.

This is strange, for at first sight, all East Anglian rivers have the same characteristics: they are narrow and divided into three to four mile stretches between mills. Beneath the mills on all the rivers – Wensum, Bure, Yare and Waveney – the current is streaming and the water is relatively shallow. As the next mill is neared, the river generally slows, deepens and often becomes broader. Only very close to the mill is there a quickening of the water before it finally goes through the sluices.

Roger Miller is now my constant roaching companion.

Heron-like concentration . . .

Frequent bitter disappointments . . .

Final fantastic rewards!

All the rivers are seemingly equally rich, and yet they do react differently. In what does this obvious character difference between the Bure and the Wensum lie? Possibly it is the fact that the Wensum is fed principally by streams and tributaries running off the land, whereas the Upper Bure relies primarily for supply from deep springs in the chalk. This water tends to keep temperatures down in summer, but perhaps to force them up, or at least keep them more stable in winter. Such subtle changes mean a lot to a roach man . . .

The two major approaches to the Norfolk rivers are trotting, which will be dealt with shortly by John Wilson, and legering. Though the joke that I do not own a float is a cruel one, it is true that the majority of my East Anglian river fish have come on leger.

There are several reasons for this. A lot of my fishing is done at night when even a betafloat is hard to see. Even in the better light, the weather is often bitterly cold. My sessions are long and very few bites are expected. I doubt whether I could keep my discipline in such circumstances, trotting and retrotting a float. Finally, I have a strong feeling that the bulk of big fish generally prefer a bait anchored on the bottom.

A massive roach taken hours after darkness had fallen.

I will describe my gear, although it is pretty standard. I am not a tackle innovator – rather, it is my belief that a knowledge of the fish and its habits really counts.

My quivertipping rod is an adapted glass Persuader of 10ft. For short-range butt indicator legering, I use the Persuader without the quiver attachment. For longer range – perhaps across to a bay – or in a deep hole – I will sometimes use a 12ft roach rod with a butt indicator. This picks up line rather better than the shorter Persuader, yet is gentle enough not to crack off on the strike.

Reels are invariably Mitchells. Line is almost always 3lb Maxima – generally straight through to the hook. Bait is nearly always bread in one form or another. Hooks are generally Peter Drennan Specimen, sizes 8 to 14, depending on the size of bait which in itself depends on water temperature and colour. The warmer and cloudier the river, the larger the piece of flake or crust tends to be.

When the water is slack enough for a butt indicator, I now generally use a monkey climber rather than a bobbin. If it is to be a night session, an Optonic will take the place of a front rod rest. I prefer to use a butt indicator

Roger Miller legers with butt indicator as a Bure night draws in.

whenever possible. I feel this gives shy fish that little bit more slack line, and hence confidence, when taking a bait. There are, however, many times in a winter push, when a quivertip is unavoidable.

My terminal rigs will be either link leger or paternoster. I do not think it matters much which, providing the weight is adequate to hold bottom. More vital is the hook length. I generally start with about 18in and experiment, should, disaster of disasters, a bite be missed.

Bites from big roach on quiver or monkey tend to be of the same type. The most common will be a twitch on either tip or butt indicator. This, I believe, is when the bait is sucked into the roach's lips. There follows a pause; this is when the bait is inspected. A strike now would pull the bait away from the fish. Ten seconds could go by, and then the roach mouths the bait properly and generally moves away. The result is a thump on the tip or the monkey at the rod butt. Either should be unmissable.

Of course, there are days when this does not happen. If any twitch or drop back does not materialise, it pays to strike at the next. I can remember when I have struck on the merest suspicion and the rod has hooped over.

All this is basic stuff. I repeat, what I am trying to do is to understand the

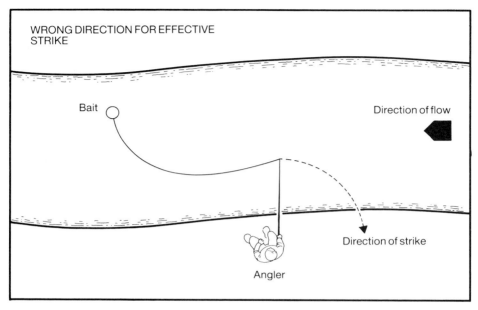

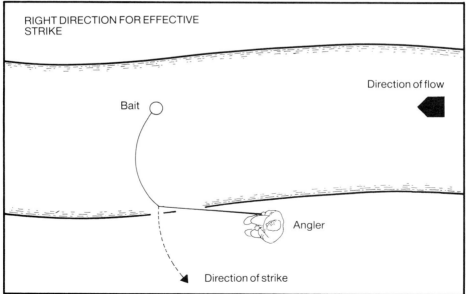

Roger Miller's quivertip set up.

fish themselves. We are talking about long, thinly populated lengths of river, where the big roach are shy, not so much of gear as of disturbances, and at best often feed only for short stretches each day. It is to read their movements that I apply most of my energies and thoughts. This is not easy. From October onwards, the rivers colour up and fish spotting is restricted to those dawns or dusks when fish might roll. Catching fish is a more reliable guide, but when twenty or thirty blank sessions are not unusual, patterns are hard to define!

A description of a stretch of the Wensum I know well, and the fishes' movements along it in 1975–76, and again a decade later in 1985–86, might provide some useful lessons. In the 1970s, the upstream, quicker stretch generally fished poorly for better roach; 95 per cent of fish caught there were small fish. Big roach did pass through, undoubtedly – the otter-eaten remains of a near three-pounder testify to that – but as a general rule, I do not believe they stayed there long.

Not until a mile and a half downstream, where the effluent discharge was reached, did big fish turn up in quantity. The half mile beneath the outflow was almost constantly patrolled by roach of 1lb 14oz and heavier. There was periodic movement along this stretch, and groups of roach wandered, grazing rather like sheep on a field. Before autumn rains obscured the view, it was not unusual to see a recognisable shoal move half a mile over two days, or if alarmed, more than that.

Around mid-January, many of these roach began to migrate a mile or so downstream, towards the deeper, slower water above the mill. Not all the good roach went, but from my studies, most of the very largest did. It was in the half-mile above the sluices that I contacted the best fish of that season. Fish of 2lb 8oz and above were the norm. Small roach were rare.

This late season migration was typical roach behaviour on all the rivers at that time. Great catches were made historically in the late season in these areas – witness Jack Fitt's legendary catch of twenty-six two-pounders above Bintry Mill in the 1960s.

The movement I have described was, I believe, standard on most of these rivers until the late 1970s. But see how things have changed in the 1980s.

In 1985–86, the pattern of roach movement was totally reversed. What fish there were, were now located above the outflow of effluent rather than below it. Apart from chub, the lowest reaches proved to be barren. The knowledge I carried with me from the 1970s was to be worse than useless. It was misleading, and over forty sessions were wasted on the bottom two miles of the stretch. Obviously, something had happened and the variables need to be discussed.

Chris Turnbull strikes into a fish.

The roach boils and comes towards a waiting net.

It lies safe in the deep mesh.

The emergence of a few small chub in the stretch, I think, can be discounted. I do not think there are nearly enough to bully the roach out of their normal patterns. The fact that the numbers of roach have dropped considerably is not important either. Surely the few big fish left should behave in the same way as before.

I believe the effluent outfall itself is half the key. Where it once was an attractor for the roach, it now seems to repel them. Years of added effluent now coat the bed. Noxious gas bubbles rise continually at times, and I believe the whole area has, over the extra decade, become soured. Furthermore, with the growth of surrounding villages into small towns, the amount of effluent itself has greatly increased. The river's ecology has changed and, with that, so have the habits of the handful of surviving fish.

The traditional bottom stretches are less welcoming in another way. Once the mill sluices were operated by the millers – country men, who knew the river, loved it and did not run it off faster than it needed. Therefore, apart from winter floods, the gates were never wide open and a slow flow was standard. Today, the millers have gone, but the mills remain as expensive abodes for the rich city dwellers who do not understand the river.

At 2lb 7oz, it represents the ultimate reward for a hard winter's day.

A 2lb 8oz roach taken in
the stillwater, just above a
mill.

They are afraid of it, and when the rains start in October or November, the sluices are flung open *and left open until spring*. The once deep, slack water is transformed. It is too fast for big roach, and they must move. So it was in 1985–86 that all the big roach caught, four to my knowledge, came in the mile beneath the mill. Change had been forced upon the few survivors of the 1970s heyday.

If further proof of this hypothesis is needed, let us take the case of Bintry Mill. There, the former miller's son remains in charge. He operates the sluices properly and in the winters of 1982–84, excellent sport could be guaranteed within sight upstream of his mill and sluices.

Though the movements of the East Anglian river roach have changed in places, I believe their feeding patterns have remained generally stable. After many years of roach fishing twenty-four hours a day, I believe there is a standard feeding timetable in which light values play a leading part.

If we take a river that is not in flood between October and March, then roach usually come on the feed about 4 to 5 p.m., depending on the month. (The earlier that nightfall is, the earlier they begin.) They will then feed on until about 11 p.m. It does not seem to matter how cold the night becomes.

This, believe it or not, is the River Waveney! On such a flood, no man can do anything.

The frost can be severe enough to freeze the line in the rings and the water in the reed margins, but the roach will continue to bite. Often my only fish has come at 10 p.m., as a full moon has beamed on a fast silvering landscape.

Sometime before midnight, in my experience, the roach have switched off. The hours until 5 a.m. have invariably, for me, been blank ones. At around first light, or slightly before, roach often roll heavily, before going down to feed once more. This bout of activity generally lasts until 8 or 9 a.m., and bites peter out as the light grows.

There are exceptions, of course, to this general rule. For example, when the weather is bitterly cold, when even daytime temperatures never exceed freezing, then roach can begin to feed in the middle of the day. Perhaps the light is now, for once, an inducement to them, and somehow jerks them from a torpor the cold lays upon them. Roger himself had two fine Bure fish of 2lb 14oz and 2lb 12oz in his first two casts a little after a January noon. One of the Wensum roach kings, Jimmy Sapey, took one of his best catches of the 1970s in the early afternoon, leaving only a central channel free for him to trot down, amongst the icebergs!

Very often, late in the season, the big roach will feed all day. In these last

John Bailey quivertips at dawn to capitalise on the end of a feeding spell.

couple of weeks, as they fill out with spawn, it is as though their biorhythms go slightly astray and their usual time clock fluctuates wildly. Perhaps, like carp before the winter semi-hibernation, they are stocking up for a period when they know little feeding will be done.

From November through to February there are days that never truly awaken, those days when a camera's meter rarely says there is enough natural light for a picture, and a flash is needed even at noon. There will probably be a drizzle and a steady dripping from all the trees, and on these days a bite can come at any time – right out of the greyness, as it were.

The questions of groundbaiting and, even more so, of pre-baiting, are interesting ones. On East Anglian rivers I have never used nearly as much groundbait as Owen Wentworth does on the Stour, but then the pace of the rivers here is slower and the fish stocks generally lower. Groundbaiting is simple. I generally flick a few pieces of flake into the area where my hookbait will rest. If I expect just one or two fish, literally, to be present then half a dozen free offerings will be enough. Should the shoal be rather larger I will double or treble the amount. Occasionally I will groundbait with

A rare roach this – it fell to a sweet-flavoured paste.

mashed bread – perhaps two slices if I feel there are several fish in the area, and if I want to feed a swim further out. On those days that bites continue to come, I will maintain the feed, even if sparingly.

I have experimented with flavourings on the bread, but I cannot say, after five years of doing this, that any real benefit has been shown. Unlike Archie Braddock on the Trent, the rivers here are little fished and though the roach are wary of man himself, they are relatively naïve when it comes to his fishing techniques. I do not feel that overcomplicating the situation here pays off.

Pre-baiting is a more complex matter. My belief is that roach graze and then move on. There is no such thing, then, as a resident fish – although there are favoured areas, those particularly rich areas that hold fish a longer time than others.

I believe it is possible to choose a promising swim, and to put in a certain amount of food each day to hold roach, or at least to make them visit the spot regularly, expecting to find bait there. Certainly there have been periods when I have had the definite feeling that the roach were actually awaiting my coming, and for two to three weeks a fish or two each session could be virtually guaranteed, in what was normally a heart-break water. Often bites came very quickly indeed after setting up.

How much pre-bait largely depends on how many fish you believe to be present – here, where stocks are generally low, two to five slices of mash, introduced each day in late afternoon as the early dusks of autumn and winter pull in, will be about enough.

Chub are a recent variable and, of course, one three-pounder could eat that amount on its own, so it pays to fish a little as the baiting goes on to keep check on how the situation is developing and to sort out any chub that are intruding.

HYBRIDS

Any big roach specialist is bound to run into the question of hybrids sooner or later. He must be aware of the constant possibility that his big fish have a dash of rudd or bream in them. Remember, hybrids need not be a 'half and half' mix. A fish can have just a percentage of bream or rudd genes to become a non-roach!

In the winter of 1975, the hybrid question burst over my head like a storm. In December 1974, I had an article on big roach published in the *Angler's Mail*. The accompanying photograph was indistinct, but suspicious enough to provoke this reply from David Carl Forbes in early January.

'The photograph of John with a 2lb 2oz fish provides a better image of the angler than it does of the fish, but I would hazard an educated guess that his "roach" was a hybrid. Newsprint does not lend itself to perfect enlargement, and magnification of the picture did not enable me to learn much from the scales.

Even so, the uniform upper and lower lips, the hump of the body behind the head and the triangle formed by the positioning of pelvic, dorsal and anal fins, shows that this is not a true roach. What hybrid it is, is purely of academic interest, but if a fish does not satisfy the standards set to identify the species, then it cannot stand as a roach.'

I was shattered. David had just released his book *Successful Roach Fishing* in 1973, and was something of a hero to me. I had read the book, of course, had memorised its hybrid chapter and I felt I knew what to look for. Though the photograph was ambivalent, I knew a true roach and my

Everything about this fish smacks of the hybrid.

reputation was on the line. After all, I had taken well over a hundred two-pounders by then and my whole record seemed in danger.

Through January and February, the battle raged. The bulk of the letters were on my side. Hybrids were the debate of the day and when I issued an invitation to David to fish with me on the Wensum and analyse the real thing, he declined. Ultimately, what the discussion did was to force me back to rethink and restudy the whole hybrid question. I contacted the scale expert Percy Austin and the fish breeder Ken Smith. I talked to the biologists at the University of East Anglia where my wife was then studying. I went to every book this century that described the true roach – Walker, Marshall Hardy, Faddist, Carl Forbes and others. I went to great lengths to catch as many hybrids as possible and look for their distinguishing signs. At the end of it all, I liked to believe, I would be difficult to fool.

Now any of these features on a fish make me suspicious of its parentage. A bottom lip that does not recede below the top one, but is parallel or juts beyond, smacks of rudd. A dorsal fin set low down on the back indicates rudd. In a roach, the dorsal and pelvic fins are virtually in line. Traces of bream are commonly found in too long an anal fin, too large an eye, an excessively humped back or rather small scales. A roach with 49 scales along its lateral should be examined further.

Coloration can be an indication. Roach often do have a bronze tint to their scales, but if this is a deep bronze then I begin to think 'hybrid'. Equally, a yellow dash to the fins or scales is an indication of rudd.

Finally, in roach the line of the stomach between the ventral and anal fins is rounded, whereas in rudd it has a sharper, more pointed edge. Examination of the 'abdominal keel', as it is called, is especially useful in spotting the roach/rudd hybrid.

Having said all this, for me, initial reaction is also a great test. The true big roach instantly looks right. If there is any doubt at that first sight, these checks usually show up the hideous flaws that we must investigate.

TROTTING ON THE RIVERS OF EAST ANGLIA

by John Wilson

Chris Turnbull, my artist, illustrator, and angling companion, said it: 'Trotting is the proper way to catch roach'. Though fishing on the lead is the constant preoccupation of the modern specialist angler, the float must never be neglected, for there are times when roach, big roach even, will only take a bait that is on the move. Furthermore, a float man covers far more water than is possible on the leger. Every inch of every swim can be searched. Not a fish will be left uncovered by the trotting bait. And as for pure pleasure . . .

I leave it to trotting master, John Wilson, to take up the tale.

I love the mystery of long trotting. It is such a searching, probing method, wanting to know what is down there. It is silly perhaps, but I really do feel at peace with the world when roaching in ideal conditions.

While basic trotting tackle is simple, I am fussy about the line coming smoothly off the reel. So, whether you prefer a fixed, closed face or centre pin reel, it should be loaded well with 2lb 8oz line, of not too stretchy a brand, enabling you to hit bites at distance. I have used Bayer Perlon 2lb 6oz line for many years and found it perfect for my trotting requirements. Maxima, in 2lb 5oz is also very good, and if, like me, you prefer to trot using a centre pin, ensure it is fitted with an efficient line guard. I had to make one for my match aerial from stainless steel wire, and have it chrome plated. It was well worth the trouble, though. I have seen so many anglers experiencing trouble, with line flapping behind the reel in windy conditions; they would probably be better off with a closed face model instead of becoming frustrated by a centre pin.

The rod I use is a 13ft carbon with a 'snappy' action, but which also bends fairly well down near the butt when playing a hefty fish. Modern materials now bonded into carbon fibre, such as the silicone carbide micro whiskers and kevlar, used by Daiwa in the construction of their lightweight float rods, allow for both rigidity and flexibility with enormous strength. This was something almost impossible to achieve a few years ago, yet there are

*Not surprisingly, John Wilson feels 'at peace with the world'
with this fish, less than 2oz away from 3lb.*

now dozens of super different 13ft trotting rods available. In fact, I often
wonder how I ever trotted all day with those heavy old cane and hollow
glass rods. For working and exploring really tiny rivers and streams, a 12ft
rod is ideal, providing it is capable of mending the line and hitting the hook
home at a distance. Fortunately, though, trotting in diminutive rivers is, of
course, usually quite close range fishing.

I shall not complicate the choice of floats, as seems to be the vogue these
days, except to recommend that in addition to a selection of peacock
wagglers, you carry a few balsa sticks varying from, perhaps, 3BB to 4AA.
The larger roach grow, the less they like to chase their food about. So if you
want quality fish, think in terms of trying to offer the bait as 'slowly' as
possible, whether inched along the bottom behind a waggler not too far
over-depth, or eased enticingly upwards every now and then, whilst holding
back hard on a big stick float.

Of course, inducing bites in low water temperatures, when roach really can be loathe to intercept a moving bait, particularly if the water is gin clear, calls for an exceptionally slow and methodical search of the swim, with the float set as far over-depth as it will comfortably fish. In addition, change down to a very fine hook length.

I have been very impressed with chemically etched hooks during the past few years and I particularly like the Kamatsu B980 eyed pattern, which I tie direct to the 2lb 6oz reel line in sizes 12 and 10 for bunches of maggots, crust or bread flake. In spade ends, I prefer the lightness yet incredible strength of pattern B640, and these I use in sizes 14 down to 20, usually tied to a 1lb 8oz hook length.

On arrival at the river, firstly stealthily walk the stretch you intend to fish (unless you are familiar with the depths) and plumb each likely looking glide. Search for even paced swims with shallow water at either end – these are obvious roach haunts – or try to locate a deep run close to your own, or the opposite bank.

Straight runs, immediately downstream of a sharp bend where a deep hole exists, are also excellent roach holding spots. Above all, however, with the plummet's help, try to picture the formation under the surface of the

John Judge practises the art of trotting on a long, straight run.

river's bed. Imagine, if you were a shoal fish seeking both food and protection, where you would prefer to live in a winter river. Surely not in the clear shallows amongst rotting cabbages and lilies, where pike love to lie in wait; or in very turbulent holes in their weir pools, where the ever-changing current movements ensure that you must change position every few minutes.

No! You would, I imagine, prefer more evenly paced swims, of medium depth and with a clean floor; somewhere where your shoal brethren could move either up or downstream in times of danger, and yet keep within the boundaries of the swim.

Once you have located several potential roach swims, after surveying the river, put a handful of maggots into the head of each, before walking back upstream to start at the top one.

Decide on the amount of weight required for both casting and presentation of the bait and then select a float to suit. Let us assume the river is quite fast, narrow and deep, ideally suited to a balsa stick of, perhaps, 3AA. Set it a little over-depth with a small shot 1ft from the hook, and split the rest of the shot evenly up the line.

When really long trotting and having to strike hard, I pinch a small shot immediately below the float to stop it slipping and altering depth. Sometimes you need to come 1ft off the bottom to induce bites, or even to drag the bottom quite heavily, which calls for a switch over to a waggler and fixing it bottom end only.

It certainly pays to experiment with different depths in the first dozen casts at each new swim, introducing just half a dozen or so maggots each trot down. If after a while, however, you still have not contacted fish, stop feeding a while and go a little deeper for a much slower search.

When the float reaches the end of its downstream passage, let it swing in towards the bank, in case your maggots have been taken there by underwater currents not visible from the surface.

Remember that long trotting is a roving game, and like your float's passage, be prepared to roam in order to find fish. Give each glide no more than half an hour without bites, before slipping quietly into the next. Be impatient for bites and do not be afraid to experiment. Providing conditions are good, you will be rewarded, although it may take a couple of swims, and several alterations in terminal tackle, before this happens.

Try also to be particularly accurate when introducing free bait. Remember that maggots thrown just 3ft off course could well end up yards away from the feeding area you have created when they finally reach bottom, and might well have an unsettling effect on the shoal. A catapult is the long trotter's friend here, and I would consider myself at a distinct disadvantage

The magic of trotting – centrepin, a quiver of floats and a lovely roach on the rushes.

if I ever left mine at home. Another essential is a comfortable stool. This is a trifle basic, you may say, but if you are to sit concentrating for as many hours as long trotting demands, you will present your float far better if sitting comfortably.

Try keeping the rest of your gear to an absolute minimum, apart from a landing net, because you will feel more inclined to leave a fruitless swim if you are not loaded down with excess tackle; long trotting, remember, is a moving game.

Fenland Roach

by Dave Phillips

Unlike most geographical areas in Britain, the Fens of East Anglia are easy to define. They are the flatlands of West Norfolk, North Cambridgeshire and South Lincolnshire – rich, arable land, formed around the Wash over thousands of years as the rivers Great Ouse, Welland and Nene dropped their sluggish loads of silt to form a vast sedimentary deposit.

Inundated regularly by high tides from the North Sea, and inland floods from the aforementioned rivers, the Fens were, until comparatively recently, a huge expanse of water and whispering reedbeds. Since Roman times man has tried, often unsuccessfully, to reclaim this rich treasure. Yet it was not until the eighteenth century that a Dutchman, Cornelius Vermudyn, initiated the civil engineering feat which created the eerie, open flatness that is Fenland today.

Of course, the angler is more concerned with the maze of waterways which dissect this fertile corner of England. Hundreds of miles of Fenland drains succeed in maintaining the status quo created by that Dutchman all those years back, discharging water from the flat fields into the embanked rivers, which in turn disgorge the floodwater into the sea through pumps and gravity-controlled sluices.

I was born into the prairie-like Fens and, like so many of my generation, it was natural that I should turn to angling, the obvious local leisure activity. But readers of this book will find it ironic that when I picked up a fishing rod for the first time in the summer of 1966, the only roach I saw were dead – thousands of them, floating in the margins of the Fen drains.

You see, the *columnaris* disease struck Fenland hard in the early to mid-1960s, and by the latter half of that decade they were very thin on the ground indeed. In those days, however, that was no great blow to local anglers, for the Fens were literally alive with teeming shoals of bream, rudd and perch, as well as lesser species like gudgeon and ruffe and, of course, some truly monstrous pike. What a different story today!

As my own angling career progressed, so my attention turned more to the roach. The lack of competition for the survivors of the disease saw an unprecedented increase in growth rate, and by the late 1970s some useful

A brace of big Ouse roach.

fish were to be had in certain waters. The drains themselves were good for roach to 1lb 4oz (but little more), but certain other venues started producing two-pounders regularly. Although very hard to locate, the big roach of the Great Ouse Relief Channel averaged very well and Downham Bridge, Saddlebow and Stow all produced some big fish, although Downham was definitely *the* place to be.

The Lower Ouse itself, from Littleport through to Denver, also threw up several two-pounders, including a claimed specimen of just over 3lb in 1976, although I have to admit that I never saw any photographs of the latter and therefore consider it unsubstantiated. Strangely, the Welland and Nene never showed the same sort of potential.

Few, if any, specimen hunters ever ventured forth to track down those big roach, and consequently the vast majority of the fish fell, accidentally, to matchmen and pleasure anglers. The exceptions were the big roach of Downham, which were a popular quarry with several in-the-know Wisbech anglers for a few years, until the shoals faded away.

I must admit that I too had little love for fishing the venues mentioned so far – partly because I did not like wading through the shoals of 3lb bream,

Two lovely Nar fish.

and partly because those waters were usually booked solid in those days for matches, and swims were at a premium. Besides, there was one venue which showed even greater potential – and that was the River Nar.

The Nar is a tiny river that rises from the chalk of mid-Norfolk, hitting the Fens at Blackborough End, from where it winds a sluggish but clear course through the Fenland villages of Setch and Saddlebow, before discharging into the Great Ouse on the outskirts of King's Lynn.

It was a favourite river of mine back in the 1970s, when we first started seriously to get to grips with its big fish. Although little more than 20ft wide in most reaches, and seldom more than 5ft deep, it contained roach big enough to make your eyes water. The biggest known fish taken was a 2lb 9oz specimen, by Paul Wilton, although I think all of us fishing it in those days would agree that we had seen much bigger fish. Neville Fickling and David Moore both took two-pounders with little effort from the lower reaches, while my best went a very modest 1lb 14oz. Looking back, I wish I had put a lot more time in, for the rewards were there to be had. In mitigation, I have to say that I concentrated very much on predatory species in those days and my roach fishing skills definitely left much lacking . . .

The Nar, incidentally, provided me with some other splendid fish, including a 23lb 3oz pike, tench to 4lb plus and, only last season, a 4lb plus chub. A few years back, Neville Fickling and I both saw a brace of dace which were real record tremblers, and a year ago I saw a shoal of bream at Wormegay which included a couple of fish well in excess of 8lb, possibly 9lb.

The roach, alas, are fewer these days, although they are still present. The Nar is not a prolific water in terms of numbers of fish, yet there are considerable shoals of smaller roach now present.

The big fish which remain are very old now, but one or two could be very big indeed. If you want to find them, I suggest you purchase a King's Lynn AA Membership Book and start searching the lengths between Saddlebow and King's Lynn. Legered flake, just after dark, was the killing method in my day.

Although I cannot claim to have fished for them, the River Wissey and the Little Ouse have also produced some good roach over the years. Again, both are tributaries of the Great Ouse and, like the Nar, flow from east to west into Fenland before joining the parent river.

What of stillwaters? Well, Fenland is not exactly blessed with a multitude of gravel pits, and lakes and ponds are few and far between. However, the larger pits which are not too crammed with all manner of small fish have turned up some good roach and still do. My own personal best, weighing 2lb 12oz, came from one of the pits at Woodlakes near Stow Bridge (just half a mile from the Relief Channel) in 1980. I cannot claim much credit for the capture, however, as I was carp fishing with 6lb line and three grains of sweetcorn on a number 4 hook at the time! Coincidentally, just minutes before, my companion Martin Geraghty had taken a 1lb 15oz rudd – also on carp gear . . .

The trout lake at Narborough, on the very edge of the Fens, produced a good crop of big roach a few years back, with quite a few just scraping in over 2lb, but unfortunately all the coarse fish have since been removed.

There is, however, another pit, a big one for the Fens, which has recently caught my attention. I have not even obtained permission to fish it yet, but I have high hopes of success – either for big tench or roach – when I finally get around to discovering its potential. Perhaps in a future edition of this book I will have something to tell . . .

The Fens these days are not easy waters to fish. There has been a very real demise of the fish stocks which Anglian Water blamed upon the much maligned zander, but which we, as anglers, know has a more insidious cause. Either way, the fact remains that the lower fish densities on most of the drains and rivers have again led to an increased growth rate. The roach I took (again by accident) from the Middle Level, a couple of years back while tench fishing, were averaging close to 1lb and that is very big for that venue.

What fish stocks are left in some of the Fenland waters could be getting very big indeed and it is really up to some enterprising specimen hunters to get out there and get to work. Success is by no means guaranteed, but is it ever when you are trying something new?

Comment

When Dave says that very few big roach hunters set out to conquer the suspected monsters of the Great Ouse Relief Channel and the Lower Ouse itself, I know exactly what he means. I myself tried the Relief Channel for several weeks in 1978 and gave up, defeated but for two roach of 1lb and a fistful of ounces each. In truth, I never came to grips with the vastness of what to me was a featureless waterway. I was blown off by winds that seem to come at you with the teeth of a tiger and drive the rain and sleet horizontally over the desolate grey landscape. My memories are of sodden sugar beet fields, mud and the ghost of 'no man's land'.

Even now, I still cannot commit myself to the great drains, even though I agree with Dave that the roach potential is enormous and all but untapped. I have, however, had some success in the Fens, even if, like Dave, I took something of the easy way out. Whilst he fished the Nar, I spent a great deal of time on a sister river, the Wissey. My incentive was twofold: I loved the river and, more vitally, in 1971, a 3lb 4oz roach was reported. The scene was set . . .

I began at the lower end of the river, at the Wissey pools down through to Hilgay Fen. This is typical Fenland: vast skyscapes, mostly grey and cloud driven, flat farmland to the horizons, and even the leviathan beet factory, which, in season, belches plumes of smoke like a great battleship. The Wissey at this point is broad, deep and relatively featureless. Whilst I knew big fish were present, I began a search upriver.

Above Stoke Ferry, most of the Wissey is private, and a great deal is trout syndicated, but here and there a sympathetic farmer or two gave me rights to one of the most lovely small rivers imaginable. The Upper Wissey is fast, clear and alternates between shallow run and deeper pool. It meanders from bend to bend and what I learnt from it is worth the telling.

My peak period there was a glorious time. I was on summer holiday and

The summer roach river.

they were lazy days in scorching weather spent watching and fishing the river in woods and wheatfields where the harvest flies swarmed. Even if I failed in my quest for a really big roach, it hardly mattered. The river taught me a lot and there was that nerve tingling anticipation that an extraordinary fish could materialise, one day, from the serene turquoise depth of some pool that was always around the next loop of the stream.

A lot of what I saw during those Wissey days, I already knew or guessed at. For example, the biggest fish in any shoal strayed behind the bulk of the roach and tended to hang deeper in the water. They were also that much more wary than the smaller fish, and could inspect a bait from a couple of inches four, or even five, times before a positive take was made. Then, rather like shy chub, they could move up to 1ft with the bait held lightly in their lips, before mouthing it, when a strike could be made. Such behaviour is hard to overcome on a quivertip and spawned my preference for butt indication, which will allow a roach slack line as it runs.

The Wissey fish also made me realise how aware a roach shoal is of an approaching human. A shadow, or a foot falling too heavily, and the pool can be instantly deserted. And never had I realised how twenty good size fish can hide totally in a bed of starwort or ranunculus weed. It is as though

30lb or more of fish, a mere couple of yards from your nose, do not exist. There is not even the hint of a red fin, forgotten and left to drape out in the current.

What I had never seen before was feeding roach flashing on the sand, showing their flanks in a startling gleam of silver, rather like barbel. Whether they were dislodging food trapped under stones in this way, or whether it was sheer exuberance, I could, of course, never tell.

I also witnessed the 'vast shoaling' phenomenon. On two occasions all the smaller groups of twenty to thirty roach came together into a vast host of some eight to twelve hundred fish. (I found accurate counts impossible.) The shoals would stay together for some days, and whilst they did so, the rest of the stretch was barren of roach. The few times I have seen this elsewhere have been as spawning approaches in the early spring. This was in high summer, and I am left baffled to this day.

John Bailey holds a summer-caught 2lb roach, taken on the trot.

Sharon Bailey with the first of her big roach during the 1970s.

*Roach of 2lb 10oz, 2lb 7oz
and 2lb on trotted flake
by Bob Mousley.* (Photograph
by Bob Mousley.)

*Ghillie Andrew Hitchings
admires the fish that just
topped the 2lb mark.*

*John Bailey holds two
lovely, upper river fish
taken in the mid-1970s.*

*John Nunn admires this
scale-perfect 2lb roach.*

*Possibly the roaching river of the 1990s. The River Wye seen
as it winds down from the Welsh mountains.*

One of Scotland's great roach rivers — the Tweed.

*The coloration difference between the silver roach and the
more golden rudd can be clearly seen.*

Perfect in shape and colouring, this 3lb 2oz roach fell to legered bread.

Dominic Chaplin holds a good fish on the surface.

Under freezing February skies, the Wensum winds towards Bintry Mill.

The lone roach angler settles on a deep bend to await the dusk.

Bob Mousley returns a fish of 2lb 14oz, taken during bright sunlight. (Photograph by Bob Mousley.)

Wessex Rivers

No less than carp, pike or salmon, roach have always had their heroes and their champions. Didn't my grandfather himself talk with Wilfred Cutting, the legend of Hornsea Mere in the early years of this century – the man who held the record for twenty years with a 3lb 10oz fish and who once took fish of 3lb 4oz and 3lb in a single day. The odds are he also rubbed shoulders with the great J.H.R. Bazley, who in one month took fifty roach of 2lb and over.

Perhaps these giants themselves knew Greville Fennell, Victorian author of the first roach classic *The Book of the Roach*. Certainly, they inspired Faddist to publish his work, *Roach Fishing* in the 1930s – that marvellous

Pure roaching history! A gallery of heroes which includes, amongst others, Jack Hargreaves, Fred Taylor, Peter Stone, Richard Walker, Peter Wheat and, of course, Owen Wentworth himself.

decade when Bill Penney took his 3lb 14oz Lambeth Reservoir fish.

Into more modern times, the roach has continued to inspire. Peter Butler, Dave Stewart, David Carl Forbes and Richard Walker himself all caught and wrote about the species magnificently. But the elder statesmen of all roach men today must be those two maestros of the Wessex Rivers, Owen Wentworth and Gerry Swanton. Between them they have had well over five hundred two-pounders from the Southern rivers, and the angling press has been studded with the news of their achievements for many years. They are both men who have lived their lives on those great roach waters and who have made the fishing for them into an art form. I met them both on a spring day in 1986.

Their beginnings go far back. Gerry was fortunate enough to know the Itchen of the 1930s, and what a paradise that must have been. Gin clear, brisk in pace, it was full of two-pounders that received very little pressure, for it was not really until the late 1940s that a fish of that size became truly prestigious. All that time, as a child, he fished the Avon, beginning in 1936 on the water of the Bull Hotel – once itself owned by a great roach man, Captain Parker.

Owen was, he says, 'born with his feet in the Stour'. As a boy in Wimborne he lived down Mill Lane – the lane which led to the mill on the River Allen. Like Gerry, there could be no doubt that he too would be a fisherman.

Gerry Swanton with a Wessex two-pounder.

184lb 8oz of roach! An indication of what the Stour could once produce.

Riverside childhoods, roaching on into full maturity, with over a hundred years of experience between them, there is little that the two men do not know about Wessex roach. Owen has taken the most precise interest in roach behaviour on the Stour. The meticulous recording of water temperatures over the decades has enabled him to predict 'hot' swims with accuracy. Constant watch on the river and continued depth plumbing has meant that he remains aware of its changes at every twist and meander. As an example, he showed me his diary for 1966.

This is a detailed account of water temperatures, wind speeds, air temperatures and light values that can be related to the list of fish caught and lost. Even for me, twenty years on, pictures emerged of the better roaching conditions of that period. Certainly it made me realise that any water temperature below 42 degrees Fahrenheit is low for roach.

Both Owen and Gerry are aware that big roach are often loners. When Owen trots, he frequently lets the float go on down the swim and many of

Owen Wentworth trotting the Stour.

his best fish have come in this way – he picks up the larger stragglers. Gerry saw this behaviour on the Itchen – and also the wariness of the big roach to any bait. Johnson was the Keeper there then, and fed the fish for Gerry to watch. The huge fish, he remembers, held the bait a long while between projected lips before taking it into the mouth. This Johnson put down to their instinct for survival, honed over long periods and perfected by the time they were ten or twelve years old.

What Gerry also saw on the Itchen convinced him that roach are attracted by the colour white. Anything white falling in their range of vision was immediately investigated. No other colour had this effect. In part, this convinced Gerry of the appeal of bread as a bait. Neither he, nor Owen, nor, I must add, myself, use much else on the hook but bread in one of its various forms.

Gerry and Owen are both float men first and foremost. Trotting is true roaching and they have made it a fine art. Both build their own floats. They have to: the tackle trade does not supply the degree of delicacy with the amount of buoyancy that both men require. Gerry uses a closed face reel to combat the consistent stray winds of the Avon valley, and lets the float trundle along the edge of the current about two rod lengths out. Sometimes he holds back for a few seconds and sometimes he will let it swing around downstream into the eddy, where he will lay on with the rod in rests.

Gerry groundbaits with simple mashed bread stiffened with white crumb which breaks up on the bottom, allowing small pieces of bread to lift away downstream. He puts a couple of balls in as he tackles up, and then single balls at fifteen minute intervals throughout the session. Owen, on the Stour, however, groundbaits far more heavily. On occasions, he will take with him 20–30lb dry groundbait – generally old bread – which he dampens carefully to the right texture. His belief is that there can be large numbers of roach in front of him on that river and in the winter, when natural food stocks are low, he aims to feed them well. The consistency of this groundbait is critical. He wants a continuing flow down his chosen swim, which is nearly always trotted, very often from a boat, so that he covers the river that much more carefully.

I must say that my mind boggles at the thought of so much groundbait – I do believe Owen uses more in a session than I have used in whole years on the Bure or the Wensum. *But*, it does work for him, and that is all that counts. Equally, I find it interesting that both Owen and Gerry so continually fish a moving bait. Bob Mousley, later in this section, more often legers. So do I. All of us catch fish. Obviously the answer is to fish when and how you are happy and the roach will respond.

101

GERRY SWANTON'S ROACH FLOAT

SHOTTING PATTERN

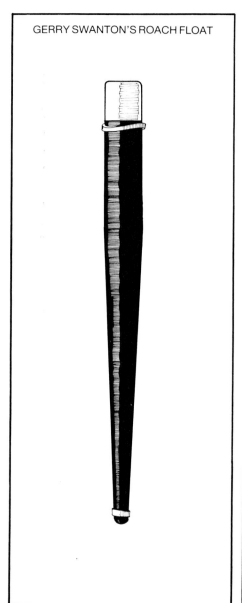
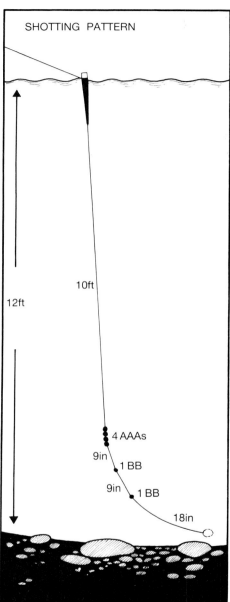

12ft

10ft

4 AAAs

9in

1 BB

9in

1 BB

18in

Owen Wentworth's best roach until 1987 – 2lb 13oz from the Stour.

Where we all stand together is over concern for the river environment. Owen deplores the spread of modern agricultural practices and drastic dredging. He worries about the decline of the otters up the Stour – and less obviously that of the water vole over the past ten years.

Gerry blames the growth of the fish farms for the decline of Avon fishing. He has seen large numbers of escaped rainbows, ravenous without pellets, attacking fry and savaging anything that swims. They hunt as a pack and vacuum whole beats of river clear of small fish. Dace they will hunt down, tear to pieces and eat in scraps. This is a problem that will not end until fish farms are closed or are far better regulated.

What Gerry also pointed out about the Avon fish farms is the amount of sewage they produce. The equivalent waste of a whole town is pumped in daily by these millions of forced-growth rainbows. How can water quality possibly stand such a burden over so long a period? The simple answer is that it does not – it cannot. The whole question of fish farming must be reviewed before we lose an irreplaceable environment.

Despite the fact that both of them have seen happier days on their rivers, Gerry and Owen still have a belief in the future. In 1986, they began to

Owen Wentworth passes on his knowledge.

prepare teaching courses on their rivers and these will prove to be popular with anglers from all parts of the country. Owen has had more time since his retirement to visit schools and clubs and to teach children and the handicapped. No newcomer could possibly have better masters, for apart from anything else, neither would say he knows everything about the roach or the rivers.

Gerry at present is working hard on the barometric theory – the belief that roach are sensitive to approaching low pressure and will switch off the feed totally at certain readings.

3 JANUARY

I sincerely hope that Gerry makes headway with his experimentation on the reaction of roach to approaching weather fronts. It is an avenue that several of us have pursued for years. With this in mind, I recall a story of a big pit fish I caught nearly ten years ago . . .

Long before dawn on 3 January, I remember noting that there was no condensation on the window panes, that the hedges across the lane were quite still and that there was no hint of frost on the car windscreen as I drove off. No hint anywhere of what was to come.

The hedges around the Telegraph lake hardly rustled, the water was as smooth and dark as an ink stain. The swans still slept like stately icebergs.

Since Christmas, I had pre-baited the shelf with casters – half a gallon a day had gone in and now I hoped that my efforts would be rewarded. For winter, it was a quiet, early dawn. The isotope hung still and bright as a candle flame and when a fish rolled far out, the ripples washed lazily against the shore, such was the stillness of the water.

No owls on their way home, no ducks flighting in. Nothing. Then, a string of geese appeared in the dark sky, hurrying fast towards the south. Following their progress, I realised that clouds, far up, were racing across the moon, whipped by a force that was so far unfelt on the ground. In the east, there was a strange false dawn, that glowed and died, briefly silhouetting the features on the far bank of the lake. The air temperature was 5 degrees Centigrade and I was confident of a big fish.

A little after 6.30 a.m., a dull rumble came from somewhere to the west. Shortly afterwards, a searing flash lit up the Norfolk plain, but it was a long way off. The lake was still. I noticed though that the temperature had dropped. A slight wind rose, brushing lightly over the meadows to the north-west of me. Just then, the isotope jumped – a line bite, but I welcomed it as a good omen. I reeled in and recast, but the breeze meant that I failed to make the distance with the $\frac{1}{8}$oz bomb.

Another roar, this time from somewhere in the Northern sky and seven swans came rapidly overhead and carried on towards the Fenlands. It was a grey morning, the birds were quiet and stayed in the hedgerows, even the lake swans sheltered in the lee of the island, and the cattle instinctively moved to the barn.

Now I drove my umbrella into the gravel as protection against the sharp, keen wind, now rising by the minute. It was approaching thunder, there was no doubting it now. The sounds became continuous, like heavy gunfire, like a dawn on the Somme in the Great War.

By 8 a.m., the wind was driving down across the pool, lashing through the power cables. Heavy clouds surged down the Wensum valley. The moon was now completely obliterated and the morning grew darker. It was now 2 degrees Centigrade, and dropping fast. The wind gathered momentum and took hold of the umbrella, force seven . . . force eight, and it was torn from the ground, ending up in the river behind me . . . force nine.

The storm was the severest I have ever seen. Thunder filled the whole valley and used its sides to echo the sound at all angles, like stereo speakers. Its lightning blazed in vast sheets that hung for seconds, the gale shrieked with gusts like a hurricane and the hail came down like a massive bead curtain. The temperature dropped to below freezing.

It became impossible to move in such a blizzard, all I could do was to sit tight and watch the world being shaken, watch the snow mask the whole valley, watch the trees and vegetation hang on for their very existence, watch the wind toss the tiles off the cattle shed, until they all spilled through the air like cards in a drunken gambler's pack. Dragons of lightning slithered nearer by the minute and hissed overhead.

In the middle of it all, I had my run. Slow and steady, the isotope rose, in no hurry. It was hard just to strike against the pressure of the wind and in the ensuing battle against the elements and the fish, my rod bent more than any fish could ever make it. The snow froze my fingers on the tension nut and the wind carried my hat away to the same fate as my umbrella, to eternity. My hair was raked back and the wind blinded me. I netted the roach to the applause of the storm.

Sharon came and photographed the roach. I weighed it at 2lb 11oz, measured it at $16\frac{1}{2}$in. It was the most exciting capture of my career.

There are two things of interest in this story. The weather was obviously quite exceptional, caused by the collision of two cold fronts, producing a squall line. The less cold of the two was forced upwards and the violently sharp demarcation produced cumulus nimbus clouds, snow, thunder and winds of gale and storm force.

It is interesting too, that the big roach should feed at such a moment, after a 6 degrees Centigrade drop in temperature. Perhaps it indicates that big fish are more willing to feed in less favourable conditions than we often believe. Perhaps, too, it reinforces the view that mass particle baiting for them can and does pay dividends.

A living barometer?

Or perhaps it illustrates an increasingly commonly held theory, that fish act as living barometers and detect imminent weather changes. I caught my roach at the tail of the storm, before the good weather was about to break. I personally could detail many examples of this type of behaviour: tench suddenly feeding six hours before rain, rudd rolling, especially before thunder. The list could be never ending.

This article was written as a reflection of my experiences that it is worth pre-baiting for pit roach; more especially, that drops in barometric pressure have effects on their feeding patterns. Then I believed, as I do now, that the approach of milder depressions could stop a roach feeding. However, violent pressure falls – or the approach of good weather, as in the 3 January incident – can bring roach on the feed.

August Bank Holiday Monday 1986 proved to be another example of this behaviour. In East Anglia, the dawn was fine, but the 5 a.m. news reported alarmingly bad weather on the way from the West, parts of which were suffering torrential rain and hurricane winds.

That morning I was on a very difficult carp lake. Never had I experienced such a hectic feeding spell there. Every carp in the water seemed to be active, and I was disappointed that I had to leave at 9 a.m. The first clouds were appearing, but still high up, whipped by an increasing wind. Now the car radio told me that areas of the Midlands were under the onslaught of Hurricane Charlie. Even though the barometer would be plummeting fast, I pulled in for a couple of hours on a different roach lake that becomes nearly impossible in the summer.

I arrived to find fish topping and had a fish first cast on the drop. In all, I took 8 roach for 11lb, before atrocious weather drove me home. I should add they were still feeding when I left and that almost continuous rain and gale force winds followed for the next 36 hours. Somehow this had conjured the best feeding spell of the summer. It was a time when no one else was on the water, and I alone enjoyed the sport.

ROACH IN WESSEX RIVERS

by Bob Mousley

For as long as angling records have been kept, Wessex rivers, like the Hampshire Avon and Dorset Stour, have consistently figured in catches of quality roach. In the nineteenth century, and the first half of this century, long before colonisation with barbel, the Avon was without doubt the most revered chub and roach river in Britain. Large bags, featuring roach of all sizes, with fish of 2lb and more being commonplace, could be taken from every stretch to which anglers had access. Local pubs bear witness to this, glass-cased specimens over sixty years old adorn the walls, reminders of a better age.

As early as the 1960s however, a noticeable decline in catches of roach, chub and dace was observed. Barbel aside, this decline has been continual, but hopefully, if Parliament takes notice, the 'Save the Avon' campaign may result in action being taken to solve the mystery.

The situation in the 1980s is that the Avon has become a specimen hunter's river, where roach are concerned. Many sections are almost completely devoid of roach, where only the odd one may turn up very occasionally. The remaining roach are extremely localised, difficult to find, and once found are usually in small groups.

The picture is not one of complete gloom, however, because these survivors are invariably worth catching. There has probably never been a better time to catch really big roach. Along with other species of coarse fish, such as tench and bream, for example, roach are definitely growing bigger nationwide in the 1980s. The Avon fish are no exception, and in general their sizes range from 1lb 12oz to just over 3lb.

Some people are being misled by these huge fish into believing the Avon is making a come-back, but unfortunately this is not the case. If it were, roach of all sizes would be present, whereas fish of around 1lb are rare, and are practically unheard of at less than this weight. Obviously this means that when these old big roach die, there are very few back-up fish to replace them, a sobering fact that always passes through my mind after a good day.

The Dorset Stour by comparison is in general a more balanced roach fishery than the Avon, and contains a much healthier range of sizes. On most sections, many small fish are present, and pleasure anglers and

The winter of 1986/87 proved that the Avon is capable of producing fish over 3lb.

matchmen usually have a sprinkling amongst a mixed bag. Other sections have fewer roach, but those present are often larger and the trick for the specimen hunter is to sort out these stretches. A typical summer feature of the Stour in recent years is painfully low, crystal clear water levels, although such times may be taken advantage of to locate and observe the better quality fish. Many roach of 2lb or more are taken each season, and as with other waters throughout the country, the odd three-pounder has started showing up on the Stour in the last year or two.

Unfortunately, barely a season passes without farm pollution somewhere along the upper reaches, a state of affairs to which a blind eye is apparently turned. Pathetic fines and the fact that local angling clubs rent the fishing from these same farmers at a nominal rate may have something to do with it. A case of the wolf guarding the sheep perhaps?

Although these two rivers contrast greatly in nature they have certain features in common. Both possess weirs at intervals along their lengths which cause great character differences above and below them. Upstream, the damming effect produced by a weir creates a deeper, steadier flow, the sort of environment favoured by roach, but in which they are more difficult to locate. Downstream is usually shallower, and hence more pacey, and although it does not contain so many roach, the fish that are present may be

A view of the Avon at Fordingbridge.

easier to find; I will come to this later.

So far I have presented a brief picture of the two most well-known rivers in the area, although there are, of course, others that sustain good roach. These are from as far west as the Axe, to the Test in the east, but unfortunately for us as coarse anglers, these rivers are primarily game fisheries and access is limited.

My river roach fishing is now confined to the post-Christmas period. Experience has shown these last few weeks of the season to be far superior to any other part of the year. The rivers are in top form, having a good flow with most loose vegetation swept away. Roach don't mind a flood either and providing the temperature is reasonable, around 5 degrees Centigrade or more, this can be a particularly productive time, as fish are forced more tightly together in the slacker areas.

Obviously they may be taken through the other months, but it is a much more difficult proposition, and unless you are a dedicated roach specialist

*Primarily a game river, the Test is still a roachman's dream.
Sharon Bailey is a fisherman's 'widow'.*

the rewards are invariably not worth the effort. At this time of year, in the gentle, often weed choked current, they will be situated just about anywhere in the river, recovering from spawning and taking advantage of the lush cover and abundant natural food. Come the winter however, they are in peak condition, deep-bodied fish with bright red fins, and for the roach angler, they are much easier to locate and to come to terms with.

As with every other form of fishing, location is without doubt the most important aspect in achieving any form of success. There are various ways in which this problem can be approached. The easiest way, of course, is by listening to the local grapevine. Unfortunately, places that are well known get a lot of angling pressure, the banks become worn, and inevitably the roach suffer through too many recaptures.

The more rewarding way in terms of personal satisfaction is to adopt a lone approach and find your own fish. Several of my roach swims have been discovered while barbel or pike fishing, especially the latter. Where there are good pike, there are often good roach, the two go hand in glove. Many a

112

time, while searching likely areas for pike at the end of a cold winter day, big roach have topped, thus betraying their presence. Returning in mild, favourable conditions, with roach in mind, will usually pay off, and if they have not previously been fished for, they will not be too difficult to catch.

To start completely from scratch on a personally unfished stretch is quite a challenge, and must be approached from the start in a state of confidence. You cannot expect to get it right on the first day, but if you do, the feeling of satisfaction is tremendous and your enthusiasm is fired to return for further sessions and an accumulation of knowledge. Walk the chosen stretch with the minimum of gear, fishing every likely looking spot for half an hour or so. Doing this will not necessarily produce fish, but many important factors will be learned about the stretch in a short time, and mental notes made. By trotting, therefore steady flow, depths and remaining weed growths are quickly discovered.

On meandering sections of river, made up of features such as shallows, deep-boiling narrows, and bends with the odd slack, roach, if present, will be in the traditional places in winter. Look for steadier water not far from slacks, or a crease on the edge of a slack, and, in times of flood, right in the slacks themselves. A lot of water can immediately be discounted because of its hostile winter state, audibly racing down to the estuary. Obligingly, these traditional swims, when discovered, especially on the Stour, will produce more than just a couple of fish. However, the behaviour of roach on some of the more evenly flowing straight sections does not conform to this pattern. If you sit in one spot all day on a deeper, straight section known to contain roach, just one fish may result, despite steady light feeding to try to induce others which you think must surely be in the vicinity. I have found, however, that by adopting a roving approach, it is possible to pick up odd fish from a series of swims, and sometimes fairly soon after moving. I used to think that the remaining shoal members had been alerted by the first capture, but subsequent observations have made me feel otherwise.

One particular stretch that I like, because of its relatively unfished remoteness, falls into this category. In late afternoon roach will often top, but not in just one or two select areas. On calm evenings, odd fish may be seen surfacing haphazardly right along the stretch. I can only conclude that they are not in tight little groups, but are, in fact, spread out in ones and twos, hence my picking up more fish by roving. The reason is probably that as the depth and flow are fairly uniform, roach are not forced into residing in slacker areas, as they are on meandering sections, although it is baffling that the shoaling instinct does not seem to apply.

In general, if the weather is mild and the river has some colour, roach may be taken at any time throughout the day. Indeed, even in bright sunlight, some stretches will produce. Under these conditions, bites will often cease as dusk approaches. Conversely, if it is cold and the water clear, the magic hour syndrome will usually apply, half an hour either side of sunset, when light levels have diminished. Both rivers have one thing in common, however: fishing after dark rarely produces roach, a fact with which other roach anglers fishing the area generally concur.

Ask the majority of Wessex river roach anglers what, in their opinion, is the most productive method and bait, and the answer, without hesitation, will be trotting bread. I must admit to really enjoying this form of fishing myself. What could be more pleasant than watching a nicely held back float making its way down a promising trot, as a favoured old pin feeds off at just the right pace, through the rings of a light carbon. A beautiful combination of ancient and modern, and to most, the essence of winter roaching.

However, while I am not doubting its effectiveness when conditions dictate, don't fall into the trap of regarding trotting as the *only* method, as some purists seem to. To be consistently successful with big roach in the limited time available, means fishing effectively, and this can only be achieved through versatility, especially on these rivers where conditions change so quickly. Personally, my satisfaction comes from discovering what method will still take fish in spite of conditions, and not from any pleasure gained from persisting to use one particular technique, irrespective of whether it will work or not. If the temperature is low, and roach are not feeding confidently, or a strong wind is making correct trotting presentation almost impossible, it is more efficient and makes more sense to fish a static bottom bait.

It is probably due to many years of barbel fishing that I now use feeders almost exclusively for baiting a swim when bottom fishing these rivers for roach. Observing the reactions of various species (not just barbel) to accurately positioned loose feed, is to me proof enough of their effectiveness. Introducing mashed bread by hand is fine for trotting where the intention is to feed a strip of water some twenty yards long with slowly sinking particles. When fishing a static bait, however, keeping a tight area of feed in precisely the same location as the hookbait is vital, especially where few roach are present, and accurate casting is imperative. The only way to achieve this in fast water is by bait dropper or swimfeeder, and for roach fishing, the feeder suits the purpose admirably.

When conditions are suitable for bread, that is, some colour with temperature around, or slightly above, 5 degrees Centigrade, a ½in long, open-ended feeder can be really effective in feeding accurately, little and

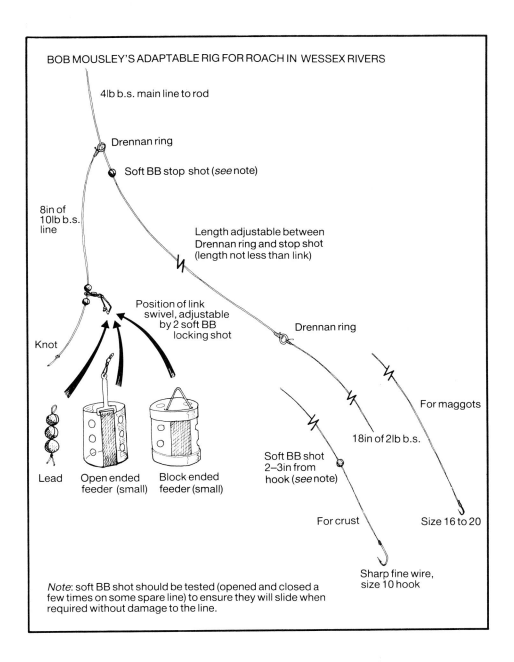

BOB MOUSLEY'S ADAPTABLE RIG FOR ROACH IN WESSEX RIVERS

4lb b.s. main line to rod

Drennan ring

Soft BB stop shot (*see* note)

8in of 10lb b.s. line

Length adjustable between Drennan ring and stop shot (length not less than link)

Position of link swivel, adjustable by 2 soft BB locking shot

Knot

Drennan ring

For maggots

18in of 2lb b.s.

Lead | Open ended feeder (small) | Block ended feeder (small)

Soft BB shot 2–3in from hook (*see* note)

For crust | Size 16 to 20

Sharp fine wire, size 10 hook

Note: soft BB shot should be tested (opened and closed a few times on some spare line) to ensure they will slide when required without damage to the line.

often. I use mashed bread with no added dry groundbait for stiffening. The consistency should be such that it will just about stay in the feeder during casting and sinking, and will then spread out in a small slick on the bottom, rather than staying in a solid plug. The feeder is attached to the line via a Drennan ring and adjustable length nylon link. The link swivel enables the feeder to be removed quickly when there is a danger of too much loose feed being introduced. If bits of rubbish and weed are fouling the line, causing frequent recasting, the swim may well become overfed, so the feeder may be substituted for an appropriate lead, perhaps every other cast. The adjustable length nylon link is important where different types of swim are to be encountered. In slacker swims, a 6–8in link is fine, but in heavier flow, especially at close range, a link can be disastrous. It then positively becomes a paternoster, causing the hooklength to wave about in the current a few inches off bottom, scaring fish. I have observed this happening enough times while barbel fishing in clear water to convince me.

In my experience of bottom fishing pacey roach swims, crust makes a more reliable bait than flake. It has a more dense composition, so will stay on better than flake, especially when roach are being finicky. Constant striking at twitches, rebaiting with flake, and recasting, will unnecessarily prick and spook fish. I use small cubes cut from the side of a sliced loaf and then squeezed between thumb and forefinger to expel the air before hooking. For this size of bait, a fine wire size 10 or 8 is ideal, coupled with a long hooklength of 3ft or so. A BB shot, 2–3in from the hook to anchor bait and line down, completes the rig.

If the water is too clear or the temperature is low and bread is losing its effectiveness, a change to maggots or casters will sometimes start producing fish again. Maggots are often scorned by roach men as a big fish bait, but if presented correctly, at the right time, will produce when bread fails. This is especially so on the Avon, where, as already explained, the majority of roach present are specimens anyway. A single or double maggot on anything from a size 16 down to a 20, depending on feeding confidence, with a long hook length, can be deadly when used in conjunction with a small blockfeeder, again to keep the loose feed in a tight area. This style of roaching is reminiscent of barbel fishing. When bites occur, the quiver thrashes around, as a fish invariably hooks itself and bolts off downstream. There is nothing clever about hitting bits, but what counts is getting the presentation right and the fish feeding confidently in a confined area in the first place.

Soft rods are a must for roach fishing these rivers, as lightly hooked fish are common, and stiff actioned rods definitely result in more lost fish

John Bailey fishes the Royalty in summer 1986.

through hook pull-outs in the heavy current. For quivertipping, I use an 11ft through-actioned 1lb TC hollow glass rod with 4lb BS main line. I have heard it said that lost fish are due to hooks not striking home, but on these rivers I do not feel this theory applies, especially with the use of modern, chemically sharpened hooks. Current drag on the line will set the hook without even striking, as I have already explained; when bottom fishing pacey swims, roach invariably hook themselves, effectively a bolt rig.

Because of this light hook-hold problem, I now use a spliced tip 13ft carbon when trotting (with 3lb BS main line), which has the added advantage of enabling the use of really light hooklengths, 1lb BS in certain cases, when the water is on the clear side. Generally I use 2lb BS hooklengths for trotting and bottom fishing, and have yet to be broken by a roach, even when playing fish in fast currents. If chub are present, I prefer to risk losing the odd one or two rather than compromise the roach tackle. The lighter the line you can get away with, the better bait presentation will be, and therefore the better the end result.

This, then, is roach fishing on Wessex rivers in the 1980s as I have found it. In the remaining years of this decade, if roach continue to grow as they have over the last few years, I would not be surprised to see fish around the 3lb 8oz mark showing up. After all, the Norfolk rivers have already produced a magnificent fish of 3lb 10oz for John Bailey, so who is to say where it will end. Personally, I would like nothing better than to see a new record come from a river.

Yorkshire Roaching Past and Present

by Kevin Clifford

Yorkshire has always had a reputation for big roach. This is perhaps not surprising with such an adaptable fish, and unlike some of our coarse fish species, its growth is not specifically dependent upon the higher water temperatures enjoyed further south. Indeed, it could be argued that the finest big roach fishing ever known in this country was experienced at Yorkshire's Hornsea Mere. The county's largest inland water, covering about 470 acres, with the majority of it less than 5ft deep, it has long been known for the quality of its fish stocks. Records showing the value of the fishing go back to 1260 and between 1888 and 1891 the Mere was opened up to season permit holders. From the latter date until 1915 access was restricted to a handful of syndicate members who invariably fished only for the pike between late October and mid-March. The discovery of the big roach occurred with an unusual summer visit by Wilfred Cutting in August 1915. It was, of course, too early in the season for Mr James Holmes, the fishing lessee and boat proprietor, to have his normal stock of livebaits, so Mr Cutting collected some large lobworms from under some timber baulks. Fishing in the deeper water near Swan Island, he was soon amongst a shoal of specimen roach and Hornsea's secret was out!

For the remainder of that season, and for several following seasons, roach over 2lb were commonplace. Wilf Cutting had many great catches, some of which were: eight fish that averaged 2lb 5oz, eleven fish weighing 28lb, and eighteen fish that totalled 43lb. This last catch was made the day before Yorkshire's most famous angler, J.H.R. Bazley, made his first visit to the Mere. Bazley was astonished as he viewed the catch, which included three fish over 3lb. A month later, Wilf Cutting landed his 3lb 10oz roach, which held the British record until bettered by Bill Penney's fish in 1938.

Bazley had some tremendous catches during this period, accounting for over fifty 2lb plus fish in a single month. He never quite managed a three-pounder though, his best weighing 2lb 15½oz. In 1915, Mr E.

Hornsea Mere roach taken by Alf Sonley. The smallest was 2lb 4oz and the largest 2lb 12oz.

Kempsey had 19 fish totalling 44lb 8oz, the best fish also 2lb 15½oz. July 1920 saw Mr Herbert Field, of Hull, and his friend Mr G. Tether, catch 63 roach weighing 126lb. During the 1930s there were fewer reports of big roach from Hornsea, although they were undoubtedly still present. For instance, a catch of 24 fish, taken in 1934 by one of the then 25 syndicate members, weighed just over 60lb. Its decline appears to have accelerated after the Second World War.

In 1962 angling on the Mere became available to the general public, but before this only a very limited amount of bank space around the boathouse was open to day ticket fishing. Just prior to this, in the winter of 1959, I fished the Mere for the very first time. The concentration of roach around the boat jetties was quite astonishing. The depth of water was some 3ft, yet the water literally boiled as hundreds of thousands of roach seemed intent on cramming themselves into the smallest possible area of water. Catches were colossal, and I remember on one occasion becoming so bored with the ease of capture, that my pal and I engaged in a competition to see who could catch the most fish on a bare hook.

For all these huge catches, I cannot recall a fish approaching 1lb in weight being caught at that time. Ernest Merritt, the well-known Yorkshire angler, fished Hornsea during the early 1960s exclusively in search of big roach. He

In July 1920, Herbert Field of Hull and his friend G. Tether, caught and retained 63 roach weighing 126lb. This is a copy of a postcard made at the time.

spent six years, fishing most weekends and holidays, yet the largest roach he caught weighed 10½oz. In fact, he only caught six over 8oz. However, the cycle of big roach appears to have returned. Fish over 2lb have genuinely been landed during the last few years, with the best authenticated fish weighing 2lb 10oz.

However, I don't expect that we shall ever see another period of roach fishing like that experienced by Wilf Cutting and his friends between 1915 and 1920. Too many factors have changed, not least the vast increase in activity caused by sailing and pleasure boating, which did not exist in the past, but I believe that the potential for big roach is the best it has been in my lifetime.

Although Hornsea Mere stands out as Yorkshire's finest ever big roach water, there have been other fisheries which have produced fish of a very high standard. Of the major Yorkshire rivers, the Ure and the Wharfe have the best record in recent years. During the late 1970s, mostly through the winter periods, big roach were numerous around Boroughbridge and

A superb-looking fish from the River Aire.

Dunsforth on the Yorkshire Ure. In 1979, Steve Hall had 80lb of big roach, including eleven fish over 2lb, with the biggest roach weighing 2lb 9oz. These fish came from just above the weir at Boroughbridge, near Langthorpe. In February 1977, John Layfield, fishing in an *Angling Times* Winter League match, caught five roach over 2lb, up to a superb 2lb 12oz from Dunsforth. Many other catches of big roach were also reported around this time, but since about 1980 they seem to have disappeared. The Yorkshire Derwent, once the best bet for a 2lb river roach from the county, has shown a marked lack of big roach since about 1970. However, there are pockets of big roach still to be had, mostly off the beaten track from what is Yorkshire's most mysterious and least known river.

Nowadays, the best opportunity for a 2lb roach is probably offered by various stillwaters in the county, or the waterways rising out of the Driffield chalk wolds, the River Hull and the closely associated Barmston Drain. Both these fisheries held some truly monstrous roach, but sadly they have been ravaged by the detrimental effects of savage land drainage schemes, merciless abstractions, by vigorous weed cutting policies; and by a gutless attitude by the Water Authority over the enforcement of legal consents and statutory safeguards, relating to the development of various trout farms on the upper reaches. However, some big roach still remain, and can be caught by anyone prepared to make the effort.

During the winter, the roach in the tidal reaches of the River Hull shoal up between Tickton Bridge and the Beverley shipyard, and some very good catches of quality roach are taken there every year. In the last couple of winters, the best roach that can be authenticated weighed 2lb 11oz and 2lb 10oz. The Barmston Drain offers roach of a similar potential, but my best results have come during summer, after dark. Laying on with breadflake, using a betalight, has produced a lot of big roach for myself and several acquaintances. The best part of the drain appears to be in the middle reaches around the Wilfholme pumping station, and fish up to 2lb 12oz have been caught recently.

Roach Fishing in the Thames and its Tributaries

by John E. Cadd

I have fished for roach on many English and Irish rivers, but the ones that hold the most fascination for me are the Thames and its tributaries, such as the Windrush, Cherwell and Evenlode, which I regularly fish. These four are, in my opinion, moody rivers, very much influenced by weather conditions, especially where roach are concerned.

The Thames fishes superbly for large roach in drought conditions. Examples of this were in 1975 and 1976, and since then few drought conditions have prevailed. It seems that the more the Thames becomes a stationary canal, the more roach feed, both day and night, especially at night.

Taking the Windrush into account, I have found that this river sometimes fishes well after Christmas. It needs plenty of water to liven it up and the water needs to be a greeny-blue colour such as you get in winter. Its roach population, I hasten to add, has declined rapidly in size and number over the last five years. Ten years ago, the Windrush fished well all season for roach. My theory as to why it does not now, is that water abstraction from boreholes sunk in the Cotswolds, fracturing chalk veins and making the river's upstream underground springs run an off-white colour, taint the river from source, so as to sour it right to its confluence with the Thames at Newbridge. It is therefore only after a winter spate, generally after Christmas, that the river takes on a nice colour, inducing the roach to feed.

The Cherwell is indeed a winter river, famed for its chub and neglected for its roach. It is primarily a bread, cheese and caster water that responds as well on the float as on the lead. The roach run large: fish of 2lb and more are always on the cards, although the average size is a little over 1lb, but nevertheless increasing. The stretches I favour are the ones just upstream of Oxford that run through the University Parks. One of the best upstream stretches near Banbury was polluted a few years ago, dealing a massive blow to specimen roach fishing.

My predictions for Cherwell roach fishing for the coming years are that the river will remain an excellent fishery, so long as we have no more pollutions such as that at Banbury, which wiped out fish stocks as far downstream as Flights Mill.

The Evenlode is a river that is little spoken of, but it holds some very large roach. The best fishing for them is round the Charlbury area. This river, similar in nature to the Windrush in size and depth, fishes well all the year round, but again most of the 2lb plus specimens are caught at the latter end of the season when more of the river becomes weed free. This river, in my opinion, is improving all the time for large roach, making prospects excellent for the coming years.

My prediction is that most of the rivers I have mentioned will improve overall for large roach, the only exception being the Windrush. These improvements will be, I hope, maintained until the 1990s, just as long as the

*John Cadd holds two
Thames two-pounders.*

125

Thames Water Authority fulfils its obligations to angling to maintain and promote water quality.

MY APPROACH TO THAMES ROACH FISHING

In my opinion, specimen hunting for large Thames roach of 2lb and over is the most difficult task on the Thames. As many anglers will know, I have fished the Thames for many years and have caught many large roach; what they don't know is that half of them were caught by accident while specimen hunting for other species. The other half were caught by design, or, should I say, caught from the lessons learned accidentally while after other species.

In all I have taken 32 2lb plus specimen Thames roach, topped by a personal best fish of 3lb 1oz, caught on an evening barbel session. Many of my other 2lb fish were caught when fishing for large Thames bream, and three of around 2lb 8oz were even taken when I was fishing for Thames carp.

A subtle approach can be adopted to catch these 'red finned rod benders', by specimen hunting for other species. I am almost certain that the location of large Thames fish that live compatibly with roach is also the area in which to catch a roach of your dreams.

The best time to locate Thames roach alone in large shoals, with the emphasis on quality uppermost in the specimen hunter's mind, is the early part of the season when spawning occurs. I'll make no secret of the fact that the place to find these large shoals is in the many Thames weirpools. They stay there for a maximum of six weeks before the shoals split up into smaller groups to populate the main river reaches. Some obviously remain. These are the resident weirpool fish and they can grow very large, mingling with the other inhabitants that live there.

Virtually all of my Thames roach, large and small, have been caught on a static legered bait – a few on the link leger method, but most on open-ended swim feeder tactics, with varying hook lengths to suit conditions such as the speed of the river and how finicky the fish are.

With early season roach, lines can be as heavy as 4lb breaking strain, gradually being reduced in strength as the season progresses and the fish become more wary.

I favour a number 8 hook with which to catch my early Thames roach, then decrease the size so that, at the latter end of the season, numbers 16 and 18 will be the hooks to use.

The rod I favour has a test curve of 12oz which is capable of casting a feeder 35yd. An inserted quivertip can be used, but it is not a must.

In the early season I always use bread or breadcrust which is very well suited for use with a number 8 hook. Later in the season I use maggots and casters. Do not ignore the combination of maggot and caster – it really catches some first-class roach.

The best time to catch good quality, specimen Thames roach is at night. This especially applies to the early months. In the daytime, the river is too crowded with boats, though this does not seem to worry the match fishermen, as they are after quantity rather than quality.

The last two months of the season see the Thames roach shoal again, this time in the many lockcuts that are a feature of the river. These quiet havens are where they congregate, after being pushed there by heavy, coloured flood water. The capacity of these fish to find still water in flood conditions is a bonus for the angler. The shoals are not as large as in early season, but a net full of fish over 1lb, and the possibility of a 2lb fish, will warm the coldest of anglers.

It is now that the float works well, with a bait fished hard on the bottom under a waggler. I use a 3AA or a 2 Swan variety. The float-fished bait should be worked against bollards or mooring points in the lockcut, as roach seem to congregate around them. I find the best time to fish at this time of year is midday to late afternoon, the warmest part of a winter's day. These roach will sometimes reveal their presence by topping. Why they do this I will never know.

With the watery sun setting and the chill of evening approaching, the roach may go on a mad feeding spree. This has happened to me on a number of occasions when I have had to pack up as darkness approaches but it has only whet my appetite for a fresh assault the following day.

The Wye

In the winter of 1985–86, the angling press carried several reports of big roach from the River Wye. At least one three-pounder had been taken, along with many other big two-pounders. The potential of this massive Welsh Marches river had to be too immense for me to neglect it.

The Wye at Ross.

EXPLORATION ONE

Accordingly, in the summer of 1986, I set out on a River Wye investigation that took me from its tidal reaches as far as Ross. I travelled slowly, talking, walking and fishing as I went, trying to build up some picture of the roaching in this remarkable environment.

The Wye is a truly beautiful water. Like Tweed and Tay, it rolls with majestic power along its sweeping wooded valley, where there are possibly places no man has gone with coarse gear for years. Only in a few places are there anything like obvious or worn swims. For whole miles, you feel you are pioneering a virgin, unexplored river. There is comparatively little information to guide you, so you feel any success is well deserved and yours alone. Not, however, that I had a great deal myself . . .

The difficulties that confronted me were immense. Much of the river is inaccessible to the coarse angler and for much of the year is preserved for the 'silver tourist' men – the salmon anglers! As I found as a resident, often even hotel water is denied to you as a roach man. Of course, the timing of my visit made affairs even worse. Winter would have been kinder to me, when the salmon are out of season. Again, other beats of river are club controlled, with little day or week ticket access. At least one association has a residential qualification that excludes visitors.

And finally, of course, there are the problems of the roach themselves. The shoals are localised and are not spread thickly or evenly throughout the entire river. It certainly seemed to me that on whole stretches, local fishermen and ghillies reported no, or at least very few, roach in the water.

At Ross, I did, however, fish confidently and caught roach from the public water in view of that lovely old town perched on its cliffs above the river. Fishing with maggots in summer is rightly banned, out of respect for the salmon parr stocks, and I happily legered flake on a quivertip. As you would expect, dawn or dusk, before and after the crowds, were my best times, with fish up to the 1lb mark.

Though I did not contact the big chaps, I could tell from those I did catch that they were destined to become two-pounders in three to four years. Deep bellied, shoulders thick set, colours vivid and shaped like a Turnbull drawing, you could see them growing as you held them.

From Ross, I moved out on to one of the Wye's larger tributaries, the Lugg. This unromantic sounding river is, in fact, a paradise. Clear as spa

The Lugg is a roaching paradise.

water, it twists and turns over a wide plain, forming deep bends, mouth-watering pools and quick, steady glides. Along most of its course, alder and willow have been left to provide shade and to build up rafts. Here and there one has toppled in a gale and has created a great slack behind it. In short, no river could possibly be better designed for the roach man and I knew it had the reputation for producing fish to over the 2lb mark.

It is at this point that I have to record a total and demoralising failure. It is as well that I should do so, just in case I, or any of my guest experts, lead you to believe that roach are easy. They are not. They can be all but impossible . . .

During a day on the Lugg I had concentrated on chub, preparing to seek the roach as the sun set over the hills of Wales. I had my eye on a marvellous slow moving pool that was deep and, in the shade of an immense alder, almost slack. If roach were anywhere in that river, they had to be there.

And so it proved. As the light began to fade, I slipped in quietly under the alder and poked my rod out over the rushes. I threw in a little mashed bread and set my float to lie a foot over-depth in the 6ft hole. All around me, roach began to top, just under my rod, so that I could see them clearly. All were

1lb, some looked 2lb, and one at least I would dearly have loved to have caught.

Then they went down over the bread I had put out. They threw up typical streams of tiny roach bubbles as they grazed over the white carpet. For forty minutes my float never even moved. The bubbles ceased. Fish appeared on the surface again and it seemed that all the bread, bar my hook bait, had been eaten.

I threw out more mash and scaled down my terminal tackle. The 10 hook was replaced by a 16. The hook length was reduced from 2lb 6oz to 1lb 7oz. The anchoring weight was made less, and even the float was changed.

Again the bubbles rose in silvery streams, and yet, as before, my float never even tremored. I changed depth. I twitched a bait back. I swapped bait to cheese, to corn and on to worm. Nothing made the slightest impression – down under water I seemed to be licked.

It was now nearly night. The water was too dark to make out the float and, as a final fling, I decided to leger using this time a far larger bait. More mash was filtered into the swim. A size 8 hook this time, loaded with flake; a two swan shot link, and a little isotope bobbin down by the reel, and I was ready.

A little before eleven, the bobbin thumped against the rod. A fish bored deep. It was netted and unhooked by torchlight. A chub! I packed and, as I did, more roach rolled in the moonlight. I swear I could hear them bubble their goodbyes in the stillness. 'River sheep' Walton called them. Ah well, perhaps he was the genius I am not.

We returned to find a letter from a man who had unlocked the secret of the Wye roach – for a year at least. I found his words so inspirational that I immediately arranged a second exploration to take place in September.

MR ASHLEY'S LETTER

'Dear Mr Bailey,

Roach are now found in considerable numbers in the Wye and its tributaries. I would like to tell you how I approached the roach in the Wye.

I am a member of the Ross-on-Wye Angling Club and we have a fair amount of water available to us. When I was made redundant in December 1985 and there was no immediate prospect of another job, I decided to devote my time to fishing for roach. I started reading everything I could on the Wye, and asking fellow anglers. Trying to locate the roach took between two and four weeks. Then I found a small shoal of roach, and had the odd one or two to 1lb 8oz which are common in some parts of the Wye. At last I located a big shoal at the bottom end of my favourite stretch, so I decided to fish every day to try and keep with them. Believe me, roach do move up and down the river.

The first time, I clicked. I had roach to 2lb 1oz and 2lb 9oz, but then, just as I thought I had got things right, we had a lot of heavy rain, so up came the river. That was the end of my roach fishing for about two weeks. As you can imagine, I could not wait to get back to that swim, not knowing whether the roach would still be there after the flood, but when the river began to fine down, I tried again.

I arrived at the river at 7 a.m., with a severe frost on the ground, to find the footsteps were mine alone. When I reached my swim, I found the river's level, speed and colour perfect.

I mixed up some groundbait (I only use pure crumb) with my own additives and some maggots. The rod I use is a Dam Quickstick carbon. This rod is just right for roach fishing, as it has a nice soft through action.

Laurence Ashley with his bag of Wye roach as the snow lay on the ground.

132

My line is a 4lb Maxima. The floats I like are the Avon type, as these carry a lot of shot, which is necessary to cope with the current. Hooks are from size 12 to 18, Peter Drennen feeder hooks with spade ends.

I was just getting set up when it started snowing and it was still freezing hard. The first trot down was a roach of about 1lb. So, in went some groundbait balls laced with maggots. On the next trot down I had one of about 12oz. I went on catching roach steadily until about midday, by which time I must have had about 30lb in my net.

Then I hooked a good fish and lost it just in front of the landing net; it was a roach, a huge fish. I sat there for about five minutes shaking with excitement. I thought I would then change to flake. In it went and – bang – a 2lb 1oz roach. I cast again and the float didn't travel more than 6ft. Wallop! I had a good fish on. It certainly put my 4lb line to the test. I got it in and saw it was a huge roach, but, even so, not as big as the monster I had lost.

I weighed it quickly on my Avon scales and the needle went down to 3lb 4oz. I was really shaking now with excitement. I had one more good roach of 2lb 7oz, but by this time they had started to go off and it was getting even colder. In the excitement I had left my landing net out of the water, only to find it was like a sheet of fibreglass.

After that memorable day, I only had two more chances to fish the river before the end of the season. The best fish then was 2lb 7oz. Between Christmas and the end of the season, therefore, I had a total of twenty-six roach over 2lb and one over 3lb.

My river Wye is a very inspiring water and is the river I love. This winter, next winter, every winter will see me tracking down the roach once again.'

EXPLORATION TWO

For our second visit of the year, on the advice of a friend, we chose to fish in the upper-middle Wye. Thank you, Mr Yates, who pointed out the King-fisher, home for anglers at Hay. There the owner Terry Moore is more fisherman than hotelier, and could not be a better guide to the river.

In my opinion, the Wye above Ross becomes even more beautiful. As it treks into Wales, it both narrows and quickens. Its valley tightens and the hillsides become steeper and heavily wooded. The roads are quieter, the villages smaller and the towns sleepier. The land is a place of unlocked secrets.

The river too. Terry Moore moved here because he himself felt the fascination of the river. To him the Wye has become inspirational and it is easy to appreciate the reasons. Not since the great days of the Wensum has a

Terry Moore trots caster for roach on the wild, unexplored middle Wye.

The Wye – roaching river of the future.

roach river so affected me. And here the challenges, and perhaps even the ultimate rewards are greater.

Terry Moore is the ghillie to have hereabouts. I would say that for a visitor he is essential as a locator of the roach shoals. As I have said, they are not widespread. They are constantly nomadic and only a man who knows their movements intimately can hope to be close to them on such a vast watercourse.

Even if a man sits on a middle Wye roach shoal, there are problems. The water can run gin clear and the fish then are unusually afraid of man – the animal they see the least of in many places. In addition, there is always the superabundance of chub to combat. Thick lipped, big mouthed, these chaps will be the first to a roach bait ninety-nine times in a hundred. Location, approach, method . . . the problems seem to multiply.

I did not catch a roach on this second visit. Neither did Terry; though he tried hard, he failed to produce one of these big two-pounders for me. His method was to settle on a known roach haunt and draw them in to him with hemp. He trotted the swim with light tackle and small bread baits, praying that the frequent disturbances made by hooked chub would not frighten any of the roach.

Wizard of the Wye that he is, he did not work the magic for us on this second trip. But the monsters *are* there. They will come. Believe me, the Wye will be one of the great roach rivers of the 1990s.

Scotland

INTRODUCTION

In the 1960s, Scotland's coarse fish became the regular target of the English specialist angler. Lomond was the first water to be explored extensively. Tommy Morgan's legendary 47lb pike, taken in 1945, proved to be the spur to men like Dick Walker, Peter Thomas, Frank Wright, Bill Giles and Fred Buller, who himself lost a giant fish of possibly 40lb or more. Others followed, and soon each springtime saw trails of eager young men heading north with whole aquariums of live bait in tow.

Many of those who went caught pike, saw big perch and also heard tell of huge roach, and so, in the early 1970s, I began the border trek myself, with roach as quarry.

On Lomond I fared only averagely. The sheer scale of the loch defeated me, and though I took fish over deep contours on a sliding float, I rarely took a roach of more than 1lb 4oz. During my second trip, I focused on the River Endrick that flows into Lomond. Roach were massing there to spawn, and I did well, with fish to 1lb 10oz in some quantity. Monsters, the fabled three- and four-pounders, always eluded me. Indeed, I never saw a roach above 1lb 13oz, and more and more I came to think that, despite folklore, this was their ceiling weight in the loch.

In 1975 I forsook Lomond, settled on the Tweed at Cornhill and thereabouts I have spent time many years since. Only rarely has Tweed roaching been either easy or predictable, and then only when large numbers have shoaled together, at Coldstream for example, in the slack of the great border bridge, or at Horncliffe, in the eddy across from the salmon netting station.

Here, I guess, roach gathered before spawning and the areas became nationally famous. Fishing pressure grew each year in the mid-1970s and the roach became wary and drifted away. As a result, I had to scale down tackle, fish at night or follow them to new, secret locations.

Coldstream 1977, 1978 and 1979 is an example of this. In 1977 good roach fell to the feeder. Hooklengths could be as strong as 2lb 6oz or even 3lb. Long casting was not important, not even for fish close to 2lb. By 1978,

Roach fishing the Tweed at Cornhill, on the English bank.

however, I found roach to be shy of the static bait and something moving under a float was needed. Lines had to go down to 1lb 7oz and hooks to 18 or even 20. Even then, bites were reluctant and the fish were smaller.

1979 saw me struggling at Coldstream whatever method I chose to use, and I began to travel the river to fish. How glad I am that I did, for I began to sample some of the most glorious roaching environment in the world. The Tweed is a fast, vital river and I still find reading it for its roach swims a fascinating enterprise.

From 1979, for the first time, I was doing my 'own thing' in Scotland, searching for my own fish, out there in the wilderness, often miles from any other coarse angler.

A roach swim on the Tweed, I found, could be anywhere. Some pitches were obvious, in big eddies, behind islands, in the mouths of tributaries, or along the steady medium deep runs. I also contacted roach, however, on the streamy shallows and in the very deep, fast water that at first I was afraid to consider fishing.

Away from the crowds, I found the roach were not shy of tackle and I could scale up to 3lb line through to the hook, with either leger or float

Coldstream Bridge in the late 1970s.

gear, depending on the swim. Big pieces of breadflake were invariably the bait. It is easily available, easily visible, easily fished and roach love it. Maggots are not easy to buy north of Newcastle and they also attract the minnows, gudgeon and salmon parr the river abounds in.

There have been some memorable Tweed moments for me: the fortnight when I shared the river with a seal, with no adverse effects on the fishing for either of us; the salmon that took a swimfeeder on the retrieve and which played me for five minutes and four glorious leaps before it threw me; the deer coming on the Scottish bank to drink at dusk, and the sight and sound of the silver stitching sea trout on summer nights.

I have never had a huge roach, however. I do not mind particularly, although I do not feel I am really exploiting the Tweed's potential. Above 2lb, my catches have petered out, though the river's ghillies assure me there are 'threes' – 'weighed and authenticated' threes present.

I am doing something wrong. Perhaps my methods are too clumsy for the exceptional fish. I doubt it. More likely, I believe I am not fishing the parts of the river where the really big roach swim. I have this feeling that I should be looking more towards midstream, in the full push of the river, an area I have only touched upon in the drought months of summer 1984. As Archie Braddock says of the Trent, you can fish a river hard, and only know half its roach stocks. The difference needed in tactics to take normal fish and super fish is often only a small one. I am still searching for that key to open my door on to the Tweed monsters.

In addition, because of the supposed threat to salmon stocks posed by coarse fish, roach are rigorously netted and removed from the Tweed. Some have been sent south, others, I fear, have been buried, but whatever their fate, it does not make life easier for the roach fisher.

Travelling 400 miles for river fishing is an obvious gamble. I have arrived to find the river in roaring flood and unfishable apart from two muddy ditch entrances. Melting snow water has also really killed visits for me.

Possibly a greater Scottish roach river than even the Tweed, is the Tay. I have fished it on occasions at Perth, but as the journey is another 100 miles or more, I have tended to stop on the borderlands. A Scotsman with whom I have formed a friendship, who shares my love of roach and who lives close to Tayside, knows far more about them than I will ever do.

TAY ROACH
by Chris Browne

With feathers rippling in a sweet September sun, she soared high above us, scribing circles on the sky, effortlessly spiralling upwards above the mountain summits. This is the land of the eagle, the salmon and the hillwalker. Here, at Killin, the waters of the Dochart and Lochay provide the upstream lifeforce for Loch Tay. Today she lay undisturbed, a glistening jewel beneath a rich autumnal sky, and perhaps much as she had been when viewed by Robbie Burns in 1789. Visiting the village of Kenmore, at the north-east of the loch, he wrote the following lines which are preserved under glass on the wall of the local hotel:

'Admiring nature in her wildest grace
These northern scenes with weary feet I trace.'

'Nature in her wildest grace.' . . .

. . . views of the upper Tay.

Kenmore marks the start of the river Tay proper, a powerful, majestic river whose flow is augmented by the waters of the beautiful River Lyon near the rather inaptly named village of Dull. Sweeping through splendid scenery, it cuts its way downstream to Aberfeldy, Grandtully, and is joined by the River Tummel below the village of Logierait. Continuing southwards, swirling through deep satin pools of mystery, it glides under Dalguise viaduct and on past the picturesque villages of Dunkeld and Birnam. Here the tidal influence begins to exert its power, with ships up to 278ft in length using its harbour.

The difference in levels between high and low water are frequently in the order of 13ft 9in, and anglers should acquaint themselves with such changes by obtaining a copy of tide tables from Captain N.H. Lawrence, Harbour Office, Lower Harbour, Friarton Road, Perth. About five miles downstream of Perth is the confluence of the Tay with another great river, the Earn – together they forge relentlessly eastwards to form the Firth of Tay. Its journey is now almost complete; as a river of substantial volume it pushes past Dundee and Tayport, eager to meet the North Sea, its final destination.

The Tay is, beyond doubt, one of Europe's finest rivers. In 1922 that wonderful lady Miss G.W. Ballantyne landed, on rod and line, a salmon weighing 64lb. Caught near Caputh, a few miles upstream from Perth, it remains a record to this day. Every year, salmon and sea trout run upstream, providing spectacular sights as they attempt to negotiate the many falls which bar their way to the spawning grounds at the headwaters of the system. Commercial netting, unfortunately, reduces their numbers dramatically – few survive, the salmon lives on, but it is an uphill struggle caused by the greed of those who look only to the short-term economy of the system.

The salmon and sea trout have always been here, or so it seems. Not so the roach, which is a more recent inhabitant, thought to have been introduced about 1940. Some claim their presence is due to fry having been released by game anglers after a day fishing with live 'minnows' – small roach being included in their bait buckets. However, a more likely explanation is that they were intentionally introduced by members of the armed forces stationed in the area during the Second World War. Whatever their origin, they add to the riches of the Tay and can provide the angler with excellent, uncomplicated sport, in pleasant surroundings.

Although perch, pike and eels tend to be distributed throughout the Tay system, roach are more restricted. Little, if anything, appears to be known of their downstream limit, although they are caught in numbers within Perth and certainly as far as Friarton. Perhaps the upstream limit is somewhere in the vicinity of Dunkeld, evidence I gleaned from a copy of *Coarse Fishing Monthly*, October 1982. In an article entitled 'Autumn Grayling' another eloquent Norfolk angler, John Wilson, wrote of Dunkeld:

'We saw plenty of salmon and were told about the horrible "scalies", which average about 2lb and are occasionally taken, but we did not see one all week. Rather a pity really, because by Hew's description of these vermin fish they could only have been roach.'

These fourteen or so miles, from Perth to Dunkeld, would therefore appear to hold the key to the best roach fishing on the Tay.

The present accepted Scottish rod-caught record roach stands at 2lb 1oz 8dr, and was caught in Perth by G. Shuttleworth in 1972. Magnificent fish that it is, and with due respect to its captor, it appears unlikely that this indicates the real potential of the river. I always take stories with a pinch of salt and a large whisky! Many times I have heard of catches of roach being

The Tay . . .

taken in excess of 50lb – sometimes 100lb catches filter through the grapevine. Unfortunately, I have the unenviable knack of never being in the right place at the right time. Perhaps the winter anglers from Edinburgh, Glasgow and Carlisle could confirm such figures – perhaps they are myths caused by over zealous anglers or Tourist Board officials! Let me say I have not seen them, but I do believe them. One look at the Tay tells you as much.

The biggest catch I witnessed for two anglers was just under 45lb, comprising fish in the 6–8oz range, all caught on maggot fished waggler style in Perth harbour. With regard to quality, I remember a spring catch of twelve roach weighing 16lb taken off Moncreiffe Island (Perth) and four roach all around 1lb 4oz taken in four successive casts by Steve Clark of York, quivertipping breadflake at the mouth of Perth harbour on high tide.

Rumours surround the netting returns, but undoubtedly many large roach fall to such operations. Salmon anglers, too, report roach taken on the fly, some deemed to be in excess of 3lb.

Natural feed is bountiful, water quality favourable, and competition for that specific niche in the ecosystem is low. Big roach must exist, lying in the current awaiting that next item of food – awaiting the chance to edge their weight towards an angler's dream.

There are two problems: netting and licences.

. . . winding through the historic town of Perth.

Salmon netting adversely affects not merely salmonids, but also coarse fish. Sad though it undoubtedly is, the roach are treated by many as vermin, and indiscriminately killed in netting operations.

Although Perth and Kinross District Council issue a free licence to cover coarse fishing, one of the clauses contained in it is at the request of the netting concerns:

The District Council, at the request of the Tay Salmon Fishery Board, have made a condition that no coarse fish must be returned to the river and, in the interest of amenity, where they are not retained by the angler, they should be buried.

Fortunately, the local roach population appear to have an unusual knack of slipping from their captors' hands back into their desired environment before any ill can befall them!

LOCATION

'My ambition for a really big fish had led me through a long list of waters: London reservoirs, Central European lakes, the great rivers of Western Europe. Unsuccessful, it was to Norfolk I reverted in the early 1970s. Nor was the race run then; it was some time before I sifted through the multitudinous rivers and lakes and broads and I settled on the River Wensum.'

John Bailey's description of applying the first principle of location, taken from *The Big Fish Scene*, edited by Frank Guttfield, 1978, is of prime importance to all anglers whose quest is big fish. He continues:

'That was how I chose my river. I have devoted a lot of time to this aspect, which was for me the most important. It is the cliché of clichés to say you have got to find the fish before you catch them, but this is especially difficult with roach. You rarely see them like you do carp, if you do it is just a big swirl with glimpses of red, and hard to tell whether the fish is one pound or three.'

In Perthshire we have one advantage, if indeed it can be classed as such – there is only one river with big roach in it, so selection is automatic. However, narrowing down the prime areas in a stretch from Dunkeld to Perth is somewhat more demanding. Two venues immediately spring to mind: Perth harbour, already an established area and – remembering John Wilson's story of 'scalies', which average about 2lb – Dunkeld and Birnam. The vast volume of unexplored water between these locations may hold treasures as yet unknown, awaiting a pioneer to expose its secrets.

Perhaps a word of warning should be inserted at this juncture – this is prime salmon water, heavily bailiffed and an area to seek permission before proceeding to fish. Moreover, the River Tay is likely to be covered by a Protection Order in the very near future, making it a criminal offence to fish for trout or other freshwater fish without written permission, either in the form of a permit, or a letter from the appropriate owner of the beat.

The overall strategy can therefore be narrowed down to the area discussed, but specific areas are more difficult to define, other than Perth Harbour which tends to select itself. This was always my first choice, preferably from two hours before to two hours after high tide. However, several factors occur at this venue which require a personal judgement before you come to any binding decision. Perhaps these are best enumerated for clarity:

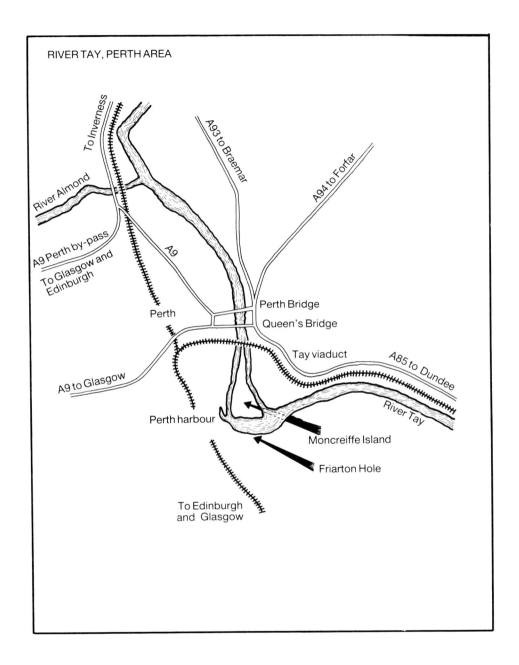

RIVER TAY, PERTH AREA

To Inverness

A93 to Braemar

A94 to Forfar

River Almond

A9 Perth by-pass

To Glasgow and Edinburgh

A9

Perth

Perth Bridge

Queen's Bridge

Tay viaduct

A85 to Dundee

A9 to Glasgow

River Tay

Perth harbour

Moncreiffe Island

Friarton Hole

To Edinburgh and Glasgow

1. Exceptionally fast tidal fluctuations.
2. Very steep and dangerous banks in the Friarton area.
3. Likelihood of water-skiers being in evidence on the main river, especially at high tide.
4. Large vessels using the port facilities, especially at high tide.
5. The recent location of waste disposal works to the downstream end of the harbour complex.

For those wishing to remain in this general area but hoping to reduce slightly the inconvenience of the above factors, a move to Moncreiffe island on the opposite bank, above the harbour, may well be advisable.

METHODS AND BAITS

The Tay is a big, forceful river, especially downstream of Dunkeld, and finesse generally plays little part in our approach to tackle. There may be a few glides where stick floats can be put to good use, and a small slider can reap rewards if the fish are at close range within the harbour at Perth. Occasionally small hooks, say 18 and 20 to 1lb 8oz line are required, especially when fishing maggot, but the main river requires an approach to match its power.

Floatfishing is a demanding but very rewarding method, but, as Billy Lane would undoubtedly have recommended, 'think big'. Balsas and wagglers generally need to carry 4 SSG or more (I'm reluctant to quote 'swan-shot' these days!). For the deep, searching glides which can easily be at 40yd range, 5 and 6 SSG may be required. These size of floats are not easily acquired and I am indebted to the staff and customers at York Tackle Shop, Hull Road, York, for suggesting a number of ways to make customised floats of this size. Perhaps the most interesting suggestion, printable that is, was to cut the top off a Drennan Loafer 5 Swan, Araldite 3 Swan in the base for casting weight and glue in a peacock quill with a sarkandas insert. I have yet to put this idea into practice, but the end product should be extremely interesting. Tidal areas require some thought to be given to the use of large sliders, as the fish can easily be feeding 15ft below the surface. Those who can master rivers such as the tidal Trent will be in an excellent position to tackle the Tay.

Legering, likewise, varies depending on the type of swim chosen and the distance involved. Quieter backwaters and conditions of fixed tide can be mastered by the use of standard swingtips or quivertips in conjunction with an SSG link or small Arlesley bomb. At the other end of the spectrum, there can be a demand for 3oz bombs and substantial quivertips or loaded swingtips! In some instances the local method of pointing the rod skywards and watching the tip can be surprisingly productive.

Hook sizes obviously have to match the bait but are generally 14 or 16 for maggots and 8 or 10 for breadflake. These should be matched to suitable line in the 1lb 8oz to 3lb range, although main-lines can be stepped up where large weights are necessary.

Baits are basic – maggots, casters, bread, wheat, sweetcorn and worms will all take fish. I prefer to fish flake as it tends to escape the attention of fry and usually produces fish weighing from 12oz upwards. Keep things as simple as possible and be prepared to feed steadily and fairly heavily. One word of advice to the visiting angler – bring maggots with you, if possible, as these are not always obtainable locally and tend to be highly priced in Perth, due mainly to transportation costs; a range of floats and quivertips/swingtips would also be worth carrying, as this is primarily a game fishing area and consequently is not well-equipped in coarse fishing tackle, though things have improved substantially over the last five years. After all, there are probably not many Midlands' shops which carry a comprehensive range of salmon flies!

One area yet to be explored, unless I am doing some unknown angler an injustice, is the use of the pole. Perhaps this is the answer to the harbour area, where the reach of a 23ft pole could be put to considerable advantage, and could be used to present a bait on a relatively sensitive float-rig at a substantial depth. Any chance of Tom Pickering or Big Kev giving us a demonstration?

CONCLUSIONS

Don't

1. Fish without checking the status of the river (i.e. has a Protection Order been issued?) and obtaining any permission required.
2. Wade, unless you are sure that conditions are absolutely safe. (Pitlochry dam can discharge large quantities of water without warning, and the river level can rise rapidly within minutes.)
3. Fish in the Friarton area below Perth harbour if in any doubt as to safety; the banks are exceptionally steep, and tides rapid.

Do

1. Obtain a copy of the tide tables from The Harbourmaster, Harbour Office, Lower Harbour, Friarton Road, Perth.
2. Allow salmon anglers preference if they request use of your swim – it is part of the local rules, I'm afraid.
3. Bring maggots and 4 SSG (or more) floats with you if possible.
4. Obtain a permit before fishing, if one is required. For the town stretch in Perth this can be obtained free of charge from Director of Finance, Perth and Kinross District Council, 5 High Street, Perth. The office is open from 8.45 a.m. to 12.45 p.m., and 1.45 p.m. to 4.30 p.m. on Mondays to Fridays.

Above all, please take care to follow the countryside code – Scotland is a beautiful area, I'm sure you will keep it that way. Happy and successful angling!

Comment

There is nothing new in fishing, as they rightly say: think of Chris's prototype for a massive Tay trotting float, and then compare it with J.W. Martin's, the Trent Otter's, solution for fishing the enormous tidal Trent in the last century. Martin advocated a great peacock quill loaded with so much cork that it could carry 4½oz of lead! A man could then trot frighteningly fast water at a depth of 30ft. The bream, barbel and roach hooked in such a flow could fight for half an hour and, with the heaviness of rods a century ago, leave an angler with an arm ache for a week.

But, Martin proved that trotting these tidal reaches could be done and, like Chris today, it does not do to be dismayed. Needs must: if the fish are there, the job must be done!

A Conclusion

As I finish this book, late summer pulls in and, with it, the new roach season. To be back in the roaching mainstream gives a new urgency to reading the proofs and I realise there remain some dilemmas that you might think we have failed to solve: should baits be flavoured or left plain? Are baits better trotted or legered for roach? Do the bigger fish feed more at night or in the day? One of us believes one thing, another the other and in the end it is for you to decide between us.

I also realise that there is little about late summer and autumn roaching. A mistake! It can be excellent. Take September and October 1986 . . .

As is usual these days I teamed up with my regular partner, Roger Miller, for the new campaign. No longer is a decision on swim, or even river, easy to make. Roach no longer exist in numbers, and location today is our prime concern. Realistically we have thirty miles of Wensum to consider and fifteen miles each of the Bure and the Yare. There was a lot of exploring to do.

We began by dividing and walking the rivers separately. We were lucky that we worked on bright sunny days that gave us excellent vision into these very clear waters. Not that we expected to see the roach themselves. Almost always, big roach remain hidden in the weed during the day. Unlike the bolder chub, they are virtually nocturnal until the winter floods colour up the rivers and they feel more secure.

What we had to look for were likely swims and any sort of clues. A roach sighting would, we knew, really be a bonus. The areas we investigated were the eddies, creases and slacks of bends, deeper runs, and any peculiarity of the river bed that could prove an attraction to the wandering groups of roach. A second factor was weed growth and type. Big roach often use those underwater 'cabbage' beds that give them such good shelter. Streamer weed is also an attraction. Also, the *lack* of the blanket weed that cloaks the bed of all these highly enriched rivers could be a pointer: our hope was that bare areas had been grazed, and therefore cleared, by feeding roach.

Here and there, then, on the three rivers, we found places where all these features came together; a good looking swim, attractive weed growth and a sparsity of blanket weed. These swims we began to bait up with bread. Each

Roger Miller delighted with a 2lb 14oz fish.

evening we walked to every one of them – thirty to forty in all – and put two to three slices of bread in each. We tried to have the sun behind us and use the light of the setting sun to see better into the water. We squeezed the pieces of flake quite flat so they would sink slowly to rest on top of silt or any blanket weed that remained in patches.

On our return visits, we began to realise that in several of the swims the bread had disappeared. Areas where it lay untouched for 24 or 48 hours, we felt, had to be discounted. Now we were left with three swims on both the Wensum and the Yare, and five swims on the Bure, on which to concentrate in earnest and with some confidence.

Of course, we fully realised that the bread may not necessarily have been taken by roach. Chub, dace, swans and little grebes were just some of the many possible culprits. Accordingly, we now started to pre-bait at dusk and check the swims at first light, in the hope that waterfowl would be a little less active during the hours of darkness. On some seven of the eleven swims, we found the bread was disappearing overnight. Now, we began to fish. I started on the Yare and Roger on the Wensum.

14oz fish for Roger at 8.15 p.m. It was one of the most vividly coloured, most beautifully proportioned fish I had ever handled. Six nights on, I took another huge fish of 3lb 5oz. Together, these roach made sense of our obsession.

The roach is a marvellous fish. It is a delight, a jewel of the underwater world, and a prize that is worth any effort.

The Contributors

Laurence Ashley

Laurence is one of those few men who has really set himself to master the coarse fish stocks of the River Wye. The angling press in Winter 1985–1986 was full of news of his exploits, of huge roach catches that were a reward he well deserved.

Archie Braddock

Archie is at the centre of some excellent fishing now that the Trent and its tributaries have returned to all their former glory. His methods of reaping this harvest show real innovation in angling thinking. He constructs much of his own tackle and goes to greater lengths with his baits than any other man I have known. A generous friend and fellow angler, he is always happy to pass on his considerable knowledge.

Chris Browne

Chris is one of those few Scotsmen who appreciate coarse as well as game fish. Living near Perth, he has the sense to sample all the delights – trout from Loch Leven and both salmon and roach from the Tay. He now spends as many holidays as possible hunting the tench and the carp of Norfolk.

John Cadd

One of the best known anglers on the Thames and its tributaries, from where he has caught exceptional barbel, carp and roach. A frequent contributor to the angling press, he is also well known for his interest in conservation.

Kevin Clifford

Co-author of the excellent book on Redmire, Kevin has long been regarded as one of the foremost carp anglers of the country. However, his interests extend beyond this. Big barbel, pike, rudd and, of course, roach are amongst the other species that he has successfully tangled with.

Martin James

Martin is one of the most courageous of men ever to have held a fishing rod. A multiple sclerosis sufferer, he has not let this affect his determination to get to the bank, or his humour or patience when there. His great qualities as man, angler and environmentalist in general all show in his angling broadcasts for Radio Lancashire and Radio 4.

Tony Miles

For many years Tony has been one of the most respected figures on the specialist fishing scene. A truly excellent angler, he has always proved to be a voice of reason and sanity in a sometimes emotional world. Tony is a travelling angler and his experiences on pits, lakes and rivers nationwide make him very much the all-round fisherman.

Roger Miller

The author's constant fishing companion, Roger specialises in bream in the summer and, come winter, in roach and pike. His tally of big roach is ever increasing and, in late 1986, he broke the 3lb mark for the first time with a 3lb 3oz roach. A keen conservationist, Roger appreciates and fights for the survival of all areas of the environment.

Bob Mousley

Bob adopts a low profile approach, perhaps more so than some of the other experts in this book, but that should not obscure the fact that he has made marvellous catches of roach, barbel, and pike from his local Wessex rivers. How well this modest and painstakingly thorough angler deserves his magnificent recent 3lb roach.

Dave Phillips

Dave has done a fine job as editor of *Coarse Fisherman* in bringing that magazine back to the position of excellence it once enjoyed. A Norfolk boy, he learned his fishing in the Fenland region but now his job takes him and his rods all over the British Isles.

Owen Wentworth and Gerry Swanton

Two of the most famous men of modern roaching, they have recently teamed up to pass on their skills to the younger generation in a series of 'fish ins' on the Avon. Both men have figured large in the angling media for years and are respected for giving as much as they take from their sport. Owen has recently landed his first 3lb fish and Gerry is moving towards the target of 300 two-pounders.

John Wilson

Norwich tackle dealer, John first began to make his name in the angling world in the early 1970s, with huge catches of Norfolk roach. He has, however, caught tremendous specimens of nearly every species and has won wide acclaim for his articles and books. Today his interests revolve around fishery management and he is a man fortunate enough to own his own syndicated carp fishery.

Other fishing books published by The Crowood Press

Travels with a Two Piece *John Bailey*
A collection of writing inspired by the author's journeys along the rivers of England with an ancient two piece fly fishing rod.

River Fishing *Len Head*
How to read waters and set about catching the major coarse fishing species.

Boat Fishing *Mike Millman, Richard Stapley and John Holden*
A concise but detailed guide to modern boat fishing.

Stillwater Coarse Fishing *Melvyn Russ*
A guide to the maze of tackle, baits, tactics and techniques that surround the cream of coarse fishing in Britain.

Beach Fishing *John Holden*
A comprehensive insight into the fish, their habitat, long distance casting, tackle, bait and tactics.

My Way with Trout *Arthur Cove*
Outlines the techniques and tactics employed by the master of nymph fishing on stillwaters.

In Visible Waters *John Bailey*
John Bailey reveals the deep insight that he has gained over nearly thirty years closely observing the lives of the coarse fishing species.

Imitations of the Trout's World *Bob Church and Peter Gathercole*
Describes advanced fly tying techniques and explores the link between the natural and the artificial.

Bob Church's Guide to Trout Flies
Covers some 400 flies, with advice on how to select the right one and how to fish it.

Fly Fishing for Salmon and Sea Trout *Arthur Oglesby*
The first recent really comprehensive work to deal almost exclusively with fly fishing techniques.

Tench *Len Head*
Natural history, physiology, distribution, tackle, tactics and techniques are discussed in this most comprehensive study of the species.

Pike – The Predator becomes the Prey   *John Bailey and Martyn Page*
Twenty top pike anglers' experience of all types of waters.

Carp – The Quest for the Queen   *John Bailey and Martyn Page*
Combined specialist knowledge from twenty-six big fish men.

Long Distance Casting   *John Holden*
A guide to tackle and techniques of long-range casting in saltwater.

The Beach Fisherman's Tackle Guide   *John Holden*
Covers rods, reels, accessories, rigs and maintenance.

An Introduction to Reservoir Trout Fishing   *Alan Pearson*
Covers tackle, casting, flies, bank and boat fishing, and location.

Rods and Rod Building   *Len Head*
A manual of rod building, giving guidance on design and the selection of rods.

Further information from **The Crowood Press (0672) 20320**